HOW RETIRE IN 12 MONTHS

TURNING **PASSION** INTO **PROFIT**

SERENA STAR-LEONARD

Wrightbooks

First published 2011 by Wrightbooks
an imprint of John Wiley & Sons Australia, Ltd
42 McDougall Street, Milton Qld 4064

Office also in Melbourne

Typeset in 11/13.5 pt Berkeley

National Library of Australia Cataloguing-in-Publication data:

Author:	Star-Leonard, Serena.
Title:	How to retire in 12 months: turning passion into profit / Serena Star-Leonard.
ISBN:	9780730375166 (pbk.)
Notes:	Includes index.
Subjects:	Retirement — Planning. Retirement income.
Dewey Number:	646.79

Printed in Australia by Ligare Book Printer

Cover design and illustrations by Josh Durham <www.designbycommittee.com>

10 9 8 7 6 5 4 3 2 1

Disclaimer

Contents

Acknowledgements   vii

Introduction   1

1   Your retirement (pipe) dreams   7

2   A fulfilling life (and why money won't buy it)   19

3   The success mindset   43

4   Finding your passion   63

5   How to make money online   79

6   How to sell yourself online   103

7   Creating your own products   127

8   What's next?   151

Glossary   161

Useful resources   165

Website examples   169

Index   171

For John, my muse

and

For my beloved brother Ethan; I miss you

Acknowledgements

This book itself is an acknowledgement of a community of people who have given me endless support, belief, ideas, inspiration, laughs and partnership.

Thanks to my husband John, whose love and support know no bounds. You saw the outcome of this idea the moment it was created and held the vision every second since.

To Dad for showing me pragmatism, business intuition and a strong work ethic. Mum for showing me determination, compassion and the belief that anything is possible. My siblings Indi, Sam, Alana, Ethan, Daniel and Aidan for your unconditional friendship, love, business help, adventures, jokes and crazy laughter.

To Melinda Samson for everything that makes the business possible. Working with you is brilliant and I am so grateful for your partnership. Helen Burrows for everything that you have contributed to this book; you are a real life superwoman.

To James Pettengil for showing me what it is to be an entrepreneur. To Denise Eagleton for my mental health and Claude Fonseca for my physical health when I was struggling, overwhelmed and broke. To Amanda Richards for your generous support and friendship and for having 'that' conversation! To Alex Francisco and Johana Te Momo for jumping into every project, business or charity over the years; you are true friends and kindred souls.

To Mary Masters at John Wiley & Sons for your belief, advice and support in making this book happen.

To all of my clients—for being the Passion Seekers and choosing adventurous lives. To the readers, subscribers, customers and contributors of the two blogs—thank you for being part of the journey and letting me do what I love for a living.

Introduction

In the beginning ...

It is 10:30 am. I am lying on my bed, buzzing! The warm spring air is heavy with moisture, and the breeze floating through my open window brings the call of birds and the smell of fresh cut grass. Just as I begin to write, a lawn mower starts up nearby, spilling petrol fumes and noise; the bliss is gone but the buzz remains ... I have an idea!

After four years cutting my teeth in business, I have formed a cunning plan.

I am going to retire ... within 12 months!

I will create a low-maintenance income of $2000 a week and I will blog the whole journey in case other people want to do the same.

John (my husband) loves it! He said that it is the best idea he has heard from me and he is thrilled to be there at the genesis of it. That is all the encouragement I need. I am off!

That was 12 months ago. It was part of my first blog, and much has changed since then. On 12 December 2009, with a business partner, I launched a website designed to create a low-maintenance income within 12 months. This would allow me the freedom to do whatever I want—I can even pack up, sell up and leave Bondi, where I have been living for the last five years, for some long-awaited travel. Now, 12 months later, for the first time in my life there is a sense of freedom in my plans because I'm not tied down to anywhere and I don't have to come back! This is a real change to my lifestyle, and very exciting.

So how did I do it? Well, that's why I've written this book, to show you how you can take this journey as well. The first half relates to retirement, the mindset and the approach you need to make this lifestyle possible. The second half provides a practical guide to how you too can start your own journey to creating a low-maintenance income focusing on a topic that you are passionate about on the internet.

All of this is based on my own journey, and throughout the book I will share with you exactly what I did to create the business and what worked and what didn't work. The examples I share are all real, from actual businesses run by ordinary people like you and me. And, more importantly, they are mostly from people who had no idea about internet-based business but who were passionate about something and willing to learn as they went.

Life is not always breezy

Everyone has a story that ends with where they are at this exact moment. Your story is made up of the moments that define your experience of living. I wouldn't be where I am today if it wasn't for my experiences and so I have included some of them throughout the book.

My early years had some complications, and then when I was 12 my parents split up and I went from living in posh, high-tech, high-rise Hong Kong with a maid, government benefits and private schools to living in a small flat in a small town in New Zealand with nothing but what we had in our suitcases. Without the financial support we were accustomed to, our situation became really difficult. Alone with five kids under the age of 13, even with three part-time jobs my mum struggled to make ends meet.

My siblings and I were entrepreneurial from the beginning. As well as milk runs and part-time jobs, we made many creative attempts to earn some extra pocket money. I spent a year or two making jewellery to sell to the parents of the kids at school, but more lucrative was all the cheap trinkets we could pick up once a year when we had the opportunity to visit dad in Hong Kong. The profits from what we could carry in silk sheets, watches, clothes and toys was an opportunity not to be missed, and for the few weeks while we sold our 'stock' we felt like kings.

Money madness!

From a young age I have seen money make people crazy; the yearning for it, the having of it and the not having enough of it. My childhood was one of extremes of being wealthy and being poor. As an employee I worked my way up the ladder until I was able to spend several years earning a good wage with lavish, all-expenses-paid holidays in luxurious tropical destinations. Then as an entrepreneur I took a risk and started from scratch once more, tumbling down to rock bottom and working my way up again.

With these extremes in the game of wealth I have come to believe that money is something that makes life easier and it gives you more choices, but at the end of the day what you get out of life comes down to your mindset and making the most of each day you have. I have been blessed to discover that the relationship between wealth and happiness is tenuous to say the least.

Today I have found my happy middle ground. I have created a sustainable income that is sufficient to meet all my needs in a field that contributes to others. I have found a way to use the things I am most passionate about to create value in a way that requires little effort to maintain, and I have created a business that I can manage from anywhere in the world. I make money while I sleep. While I am not yet rich beyond my wildest dreams, we have only just begun.

From burgers to business coaching

My background has given me the opportunity to know people from all walks of life. What I have learned is that everyone has the opportunity to do well. Anyone who is willing to dream and take action (often outside their comfort zone) has the opportunity to make what can seem impossible, possible. I have seen very determined people who were struggling either personally or financially triumph through persistence and passion. I have also witnessed very intelligent and privileged people living small lives because they are unwilling to deal with the discomfort of stepping into the unknown.

If you are reading this book you probably have an interest in creating more freedom, financial stability or fulfilment—or all three. Every one of these things is possible with the ideas and instructions in this book, but you need to bring to it a willingness to take action, and to take action now! For this reason I have included exercises for you to work through so you can find your own passions and develop them into something that can create an alternative source of income for you.

I have worked hard in every job I've had, whether flipping burgers, telesales, IT sales, event management or being an entrepreneur or business coach. I have looked to create a lifestyle that would give me the freedom to spend my time doing the things I am most passionate about, and I have found it. The result is my 12-month adventure to retire young, and that is what I am sharing with you right now.

Why 12 months?

I chose 12 months because it is short enough that you can make plans, but long enough that anything can happen. In 12 months you can fall in love, change career, travel the world, have a baby, win it all or lose everything. In 12 months you can create a complete life change—I know, I've done it! The reality is that this is not rocket science…it is actually the simplicity that has surprised me.

If this book at least inspires you to re-evaluate and re-discover your passions, your dreams and what you want to achieve, that's a start. But I will of course be much happier if you write to me this time next year to let me know that you have retired and are spending your days doing what you love.

Who should read this book?

This book is for anyone who wants to take their life by the horns and create their dream lifestyle. It is for people who are not afraid to try something new, for those of you who are prepared to get on the court and play an adventurous game of life. And if you *are* afraid to try new things, this book will help you get over it.

If you are a sceptic or cynic, you will read the book with scepticism and cynicism. That's fine, but do not expect the same results as someone who is prepared to embrace positive concepts, attitudes and the idea that maybe, just maybe, anything is possible. I invite you to leave your scepticism and cynicism at the door while you read the book. I promise that they will be waiting for you when you are done…if you want them back.

On a practical note…

Throughout this book there are exercises to help you turn your own dreams and ideas into business concepts. If you are interested in really making the most of this, get a dedicated notebook or open a new file on your computer to work on your answers and ideas along the way. If you wish to download the worksheets they are available on my website. Go to:

<www.retireyoung.com.au>
Password for book resources: passion99

The second half of the book covers technical information on how you can create your own internet business. I have simplified much of it to make it more easily digestible. For those who need more information I have included all of the example websites, abbreviations, terms and phrases at the back of the book, and more advanced instructions and guides are available on the website.

So sit back, relax and enjoy!

Serena Star-Leonard
Bondi, February 2011
<www.retireyoung.com.au>

Chapter 1

Your retirement (pipe) dreams

Retirement: the traditional view

The bad news is that although most people have fantasies of retirement, for the majority the traditional concept of retirement is precarious. The number of people working past the age of 65 is soaring. Some do so because they enjoy it, but most continue to work because they have to. Every person I know who lives solely on a pension has to be extremely careful with their money. They perpetually 'do without' at a time in their lives when medical expenses become greater, and this is when they finally have the freedom and time to enjoy their lives.

Many people live week to week financially, and unless there is some sort of compulsory savings or superannuation scheme most people do not have the capacity or incentive to save for the future. Moreover, according to the UN, more than half the 800 million people in the world's least developed countries live below the poverty line; for these people retirement is an inconceivable concept enjoyed by wealthy people elsewhere.

Even if we are lucky enough and responsible enough to save throughout our lives, our careful savings or investments are at the mercy of external financial forces; that is, the actions and inactions of corporations and governments. As we know, they are not infallible and we cannot put all our faith in what traditionally have been thought of as fail-safe systems. Most recently during the global financial crisis superannuation savings in Australia dropped in value significantly. In the media we have witnessed people approaching retirement age dealing with the reality that they are no longer able to retire when they planned to and had saved for.

Basically, whether we think of it or not, many of us have a glorified notion that we are able to just stop working at 65 and then live the dream life. But in reality, the majority of people in the world will not be in a position to do this … that is if you are still alive and healthy enough to enjoy it!

This is not good news when you have been working five days a week for 45 years, and far worse if you don't get any fulfilment from your job. There is, however, an internationally growing consciousness that life doesn't have to go that way.

A new age, a new opportunity

In this book I give you the tools to turn the preconceived notions of work and retirement on their head. You too have the opportunity to become part of the global network of people who are motivated to find new ways to create their own freedom, fulfilment and financial independence. In fact, if you are reading this book you are already one of them.

Wanting to have an easier or more fulfilling life is certainly not a new concept. But in this day and age, people who have the right tools and a commitment to succeed have a better chance than ever before. Using the internet we have 24-hour access to the estimated 1.8 billion people in the world who use it.

Gone are the days when you work in one job, career, city or country your whole life. Things are changing, and it's time we reviewed how we create value and income over the course of our lives. Of course there will always be a need for jobs, and there will always be plenty of people to work them. But for those who choose it and are willing to put themselves out there — there is another option.

Passion, freedom, lifestyle

This book is about creating a business that is designed to give you geographical freedom, time freedom or lifestyle freedom — and, preferably, all three. This is what I propose ... if you are game. You too can explore how to create value from your passions, and use that to create a sustainable income using the internet.

What this means for you will depend on what you want from life and how big your goals are. For example, if you are a working parent in a two-income family, an extra few hundred a month plus what you save on childcare could be all you need to make it feasible to be a stay-at-home mum or dad. Whereas if you want to maintain a six-figure income when you leave your job you will need to work harder or smarter to achieve it.

As far as I am concerned the ultimate job, business or lifestyle is one where I am doing something I love that contributes to the world and that gives me a huge sense of freedom and fulfilment. The best form of income generation gives me everything I need and requires very little time to maintain.

What if you could create an income doing something you love that requires very little time to maintain? Does that appeal to you? It's exactly what I've done, and the purpose of this book is to share my journey with you so that you can do it too.

Creating a low-maintenance income is a skill

If you are looking for a magic 'get-rich-quick' scheme in this book, you are going to be a little disappointed. The day I come across a get-rich-quick scheme that actually works, I promise to write another book and share it with you! In the meantime, I can offer you my *get comfortable, fulfilled and happy over time* system. Creating a low-maintenance income is a skill like any other; you must practise and learn in order to reap the rewards.

This system takes some time to develop, which is why I set a time frame of 12 months to reach retirement. It also tends to create surprising results and unexpected opportunities (like writing this book!) that will present themselves along the way. Everything in this book is possible as long as you are willing to learn and practise what will work for you and your areas of interest, your business and your customers. Also, as with everything on the internet, things change at a rate of knots so there is always more to learn.

Staying motivated

One thing I found to be highly motivating was the public decla- ration of my intention to create a low-maintenance income over 12 months. If I am not extremely disciplined I will often leave things to the last minute, especially if they seem hard! For this reason a public declaration really kept me on track and gave me the energy to push through to make sure that things happened when they needed to so that I continued to progress with speed towards my goal.

I recommend that you think of something that will really motivate you to achieve your goal. If you are serious about retiring in 12 months you need something or someone big and hairy to keep you on track, otherwise everything will likely drift to the next day, the next week or the next month. Don't let this happen to you.

Generating your own time motivators

Time motivators will be your biggest asset, especially if you are working full time, managing the kids, keeping up with your social life and spending time on your relationship and every other exciting, fun and meaningful—or meaningless—distraction in your life.

Time motivators are personal deadlines that you can't avoid. Have you noticed that when you prepare for hugely important dates that you tend to get things done, no matter how busy you are? If it is important enough to you, you can get huge results, even if it's at the last minute. Things like getting everything packed before the truck arrives on moving day, finishing assignments at the last minute or getting organised for the big Christmas dinner at your house. These things may seem impossible with everything you have on, but the firm date and the importance of the event gives you a commitment that will have you triumph miraculously over all of the circumstances that are thrown at you.

If you are able to bring that same commitment to your lifestyle business, your chances of success will skyrocket. The question is: what is important enough for you that would inspire you to be 100 per cent committed to making your goals work? What scenario would be so important to achieve, or so horrible to fail at, that just the thought of it would put butterflies in your stomach and spur you into action?

Think about this as you read through the book, and, if you can, make a public commitment to your success.

Passive versus low-maintenance income

In this book I focus on creating a low-maintenance income based on something you are passionate about which allows you to live the lifestyle you really want. I don't talk about passive incomes because for most people the ability to create truly passive income doesn't exist. Even people I know who collect a so-called passive income still have their eye on their affairs (such as the stock market or property managers) to make sure they are making money. They still do some work to maintain it.

The term passive income is problematic for two reasons. First it gives us a false impression of what we should be aiming for. It gives us the idea that we should be trying to get something for nothing. Although there is space for some people in this world to be doing nothing, it is not a right, and it does not lead to fulfilment. On the whole we humans love to achieve, challenge ourselves, succeed, contribute, feel useful and appreciated, and it is from these things that we derive our fulfilment. While it is heavenly to take an extended break and do nothing, after a while the overwhelming majority of people would start to see things they want to do, get involved in, learn and achieve.

Second, I am sure that the world would be a better place if the majority of people felt fulfilled because they were sharing the things they are good at and doing what they love to do. You know when you meet people who love their work; they are just amazing and bring energy and life to a place and to the people around them. People who derive their income from their passions are a sight to behold. It is the juice that adds so much meaning to life.

So, I will remove the concept of passive income from the picture, and instead go to work on helping you create a low-maintenance income. The key to measuring the quality of this kind of income is the amount of time required to maintain it and the amount of fun you have or fulfilment you get from producing it.

What do you need to begin?

First let me say that there is no right way to create a low-maintenance income. Businesses set up to create a particular lifestyle are not a new concept. People have been moving to small farms, starting adventure sport or travel companies and opening bed & breakfasts in gorgeous locations for years. Now, with the internet we have an opportunity to create a more flexible lifestyle business that can be managed from anywhere you can get online—and these days that's just about everywhere—with very little cost, risk and ongoing input of our time.

The costs associated with setting up an internet business can vary from almost nothing to millions of dollars. The amount you spend will depend on your budget, skills and needs. The thing about websites is that you can always upgrade! If this is your first time in the world of internet business (or in any business for that matter), you have some learning to do. I want to make sure that I don't leave anybody behind, so this book assumes you have little or no knowledge of how it all works. In doing so, I will take you through the very basics of creating a low-cost, low-risk entry point to internet business. Start small, grow organically and upgrade as you expand over the first 12 months; beyond that you can upgrade and reinvest in the business as you see fit. This will happen naturally as you gain experience with internet marketing, managing a website and developing a web-based business.

Here are the basic requirements to get you off the ground:

➦ a computer

➦ access to the internet

➦ minimum $50 for set-up costs (yes, $50)

➦ time to spend working on your business—the more you can spend the better (I suggest a minimum of eight to ten hours per week, but like anything, the more time and effort you put in, the more quickly you will get results)

➦ a keen mind, open and willing to learn.

Of course, if you have extra money to spend there are plenty of tools, services and resources that you can bring into the mix that will help to build your business more quickly, speed up your success or improve your presentation. Also, you may have other contacts, networks and opportunities that can benefit your business; these will depend entirely on who you know and who you meet.

The reality is that you can feasibly set up a business with $50 and a computer and market your products or services to 1.8 billion potential customers. If that doesn't level the playing field and give everyone a fair go, I don't know what does. The internet provides a *huge* opportunity that has never been seen before, and if you can be flexible and keep abreast of the fast-moving world of internet applications and social networks there is no reason why you can't create a long-term, sustainable stream of income that once set up can require very little to maintain.

Your retirement goals

It is up to you to decide on your income goal, and it will be different for everyone. It may be $200 a week to pay the family grocery bill or $5000 a week to live the high life and drive a Ferrari. There is no correct number; all you need is a tangible goal and the willingness to do what it takes to achieve it.

Where are you now?

Without going into every possible scenario, here are some suggestions for how an internet business will give you more options for your lifestyle. See if you can find yourself in any of these work/life situations:

> *You are passionate about your existing job or profession.* For example, I know nurses, doctors and masseuses who are in their element as healers and carers but who want a secondary focus from which they can derive additional income. You still want to work in your field but an additional income stream might mean you take a few more weeks of leave each year.
>
> If you are one of the lucky people who simply love your work, then your goal may be simply to dabble with a business as a hobby so you can discover how to generate additional income, or be free to retire when you are good and ready.

> *You do not like or are not fulfilled by your current job or profession.* If you are ready to press the eject button and move on, this book will give you the tools, information and strategies you need to create a low-maintenance income from something you are passionate about. If you want to

expedite the process you may choose to also provide a service offering that will complement your website. This has the bonus of helping with cash flow as well as giving you the opportunity to leave your job earlier.

➪ *You are a full-time parent or student, or someone who has another priority.* If your attention is mostly elsewhere (and you can squeeze in the time to start something new), this style of business could set you up to maintain your ability to focus on your priorities, like not returning to work after your maternity leave is up. Let's face it, who couldn't use some additional income? The type of business I propose is also great if your business services the community in which you spend most of your time. For example, if you are a student, your website may be designed to service other students, and parents may share their experiences as parents.

➪ *You want to retire from paid employment.* If your job or lifestyle is not as fulfilling as you would like and you would be happy to leave or make radical changes, this book may be the solution you have been looking for. If this is the case, I suggest you become a sponge and soak up the ideas in this book and in other resources available through my website. Give yourself specific time frames and income goals and be determined in your approach. The higher the income you need, the harder or smarter you will need to work to accomplish it. Prioritise your efforts to grow the business, leverage what you have and be bold in your pursuit.

There is no exact science to starting or running a business, but one thing is for certain: if you don't start you will never know the outcome.

Real life examples

This book is a practical guide to achieving what I have achieved. The good news is that everything in this book relates to things my business partner Melinda Samson and I have actually done in the creation of a real business: Grassroots Internet Strategy.

Grassroots Internet Strategy is a website business that helps small business owners to improve their websites so they produce the results they want for the business. The website was developed using all the information, advice and strategies included in this book and was my testing ground for whether it is possible to create a low-maintenance income from a part-time website business with very little start-up capital.

Some of what I will share are things that we did well from the beginning, and some of what I will share are things that we didn't do well, or screwed up and learned the hard way!

Regardless of your experience, any new business will bring with it mistakes and lessons to be learned. What really helps, though, is learning from others who have gone before you. For this reason I have included case studies throughout the book from the creation and development of the Grassroots Internet Strategy website and plenty of other real businesses that have done things well. From the case studies you can see what we did and why we did it so that you can have a head start using our experiences as examples.

The wrap-up

> The right to retire and have the good life at 65 is not as accessible as many of us assume. This can be a disappointment if we have worked hard our whole lives in unfulfilling work.

> With the internet there are now new choices for those who seek alternative lifestyle options.

> Your ultimate income option is one where you are doing something you love that takes as little time to maintain as possible.

➥ The only way to learn the skill of creating low-maintenance income is with trial and experience, so get started as soon as possible, and learn from those who have done it before.

➥ Find an external motivator that will keep you taking action and on your way to success.

➥ Although you could spend millions of dollars on a new website business, you can set up a basic internet business for as little as $50.

➥ To start with you need an internet connection, a computer, to be keen and willing to learn, and have a minimum of eight hours a week to spend on your website.

➥ Your retirement goals will vary depending on your wants and needs; what is important is to be clear on what those goals are so that you have something to work towards!

Chapter 2

A fulfilling life (and why money won't buy it)

Using the internet we have the opportunity to create income from something we are most passionate about. This gives us access to a deliciously fulfilling life. The question is, what do you want from life?

If you are someone who has focused on money as the end goal, rather than as a means to an end, I am going to give you a new perspective. By reviewing and perhaps altering your attitude to money and employment you can unleash your wildest dreams and live the life you always wanted to live. The beauty of this is that depending on your situation you can transition to a new future smoothly over time, in your spare time, or really make a focused effort to have this quickly (like in 12 months!); it is entirely up to you and it is never too late to start. You don't need to be an expert in your field to be of immense value to people. It is about your ability to present your value in a way that appeals to like-minded people and makes it accessible to them.

Creating a life worth living is not something that happens overnight. It requires an investment of time and effort and a massive commitment to make it happen. But, if you are determined in your pursuit and choose to design your income generation around something you are passionate about, the journey to achieving it will be thrilling and the fulfilment you get will blow your mind.

What *is* a fulfilling life?

So what exactly is a fulfilling life? How do you measure it? How do you know once you have achieved it?

This is the bit that is entirely up to you! There is no measure of fulfilment other than your own personal experience, and it will come down to the goals you set for yourself and your experience once you reach your goals. The lesson I have learned, however, is that once you start the journey of fulfilling personal goals, you start to get a little adventurous with the types of goals you allow yourself to create.

From the age of 15 I worked in a variety of jobs. I worked for good companies where my responsibilities and income grew rapidly, and by 25 I was in a great place in life. I had a good job, money, no mortgage and no responsibilities. I had regular holidays, great weekends, a nice place to live, and looking from the outside in, people told me that I had everything and should appreciate it.

But I didn't. I was not fulfilled. I was persistently ignoring my goals. I wanted to spend six months in South America and learn Spanish but I could not take that much leave from work. I wanted to make a difference in the world and be involved in the start-up of projects that improved people's lives, but I was too busy to get involved. I wanted to start my own business, but I was scared and I felt I was not ready.

It became clear that I was using my good job and the security it provided to prevent me doing many of the things I really wanted to be doing with my life. The job and its salary were a tangible and emotional safety net ensuring that I had a good life, but not the kind of life I was dreaming of. Year after year, a sense of dissatisfaction grew as I continued to postpone what was important to me — I was adjourning life for fear of stepping away from the safety and into the unknown. All the excuses were fuelled by the fear that I couldn't really have it all, that maybe this was as good as it was going to get and I should make the most of it. This thinking kept me trapped for years.

I found plenty of ways to ignore the urges to find something more fulfilling by socialising, travelling and having adventures. But my travel was limited to four weeks annual leave, my adventures were limited to evenings and weekends, and shopping and nightlife were the only escapes from the growing sense of entrapment I was feeling. Was this really how life was going to go? It did not seem to matter how much I was earning or how much success I had in my job; I felt that there had to be more to life. It was like I was waiting for my destiny to tap me on the shoulder, for someone to hand me the red pill.

Looking back I see that I had no lifestyle goal, no personal challenges, and that I was just living week to week, year to year without really realising that I was the only person who could dictate the direction of my life. When you are not directing your own life, things can be exciting for a while because anything could happen! But I ended up charging full speed in a direction that was not very fulfilling. I wanted more out of life; I wanted to do something I could be proud of.

The life change bug bit me in the form of creating projects that made a difference to others. I was introduced to a group who encouraged my entrepreneurial spirit and supported me in creating worthwhile goals and challenged me to make them happen.

I dabbled in it outside of work hours with a small project for disadvantaged kids, then progressing to more causes and bigger events, each one giving me an opportunity to grow my confidence and discover a sense of excitement and purpose. I was great at some things and terrible at others, but I began to realise that if I wanted to live a fulfilling life I had to be willing to take the first steps towards things that I was passionate about, even if it was confronting and I didn't know how.

What do you *really* want from life?

So, how do you do what you love and create an income from it? How do you create this amazing dream lifestyle? Is it available to anyone?

Well first you need to start paying attention to what it is you really want from life. Those wistful moments of desire when you dream about what is possible, those passions and yearnings that you manage to suppress each day as you go about your work routine, every moment from when you first hit the snooze button through to battling other commuters on your way home in the evening.

Test yourself. How many times have you daydreamed about what your perfect life would look like and then dismissed it as unachievable? How often have you had a great idea, but instantaneously thought of all the reasons why you should not or could not achieve it? How many times have you questioned and doubted your abilities? The more often you listen to these insidious, niggling little doubts, the more real they will become, and the more real they become the more impossible your dream lifestyle or perfect life will seem.

During the years I have been coaching business owners, and partly because of my addiction to seeing people's faces light up when they are thinking about the things they love in life, I have asked hundreds of people what they really want from life.

Sadly, I often hear how dreams are clouded with the need to make more money. It seems that people think they need money to be free to achieve the things they want in life and this stops them aiming for what they want now. Ask someone what they want from their business or lifestyle and they will often talk about wealth and money and material things (bigger, better, faster). But ask them what they would want if they didn't have to worry about money and the answers are different, yet very similar for most people:

I want to travel more and have more adventures.

I want to spend more time with my family.

I want to make a difference in the world.

It's amazing to watch the clarity of vision when people remove their concern about cash. Suddenly there is simplicity and dreams of a lifestyle that are often far more attainable than people think. With this clarity people are able to create goals that have tangible steps to achieving them.

Why money is the wrong goal

I think we spend far too much time focusing on money and not enough time focusing on having our dream lifestyle or goals come to fruition. One of the reasons we do this is because we believe that money equals freedom—we think money will enable us to do and have the things that we think will make us happy.

Somewhere along the way we became conditioned, through our parents and peers, the attitudes in the school yard, the media and our mentors. Regardless of the source, throughout our lives many of us develop a firm belief that more money is the only way we can have more freedom.

We believe that to have the lifestyle we want, we need more and more and more money so that we can have more freedom. So we start working, and then over the years we look for pay rises, promotions and new jobs. If we are smart, we save our money and make investments and all our hard work pays off when we retire. The better you do at this, the earlier and wealthier you may retire. The reality, however, is that a large proportion of people in our communities carry on working long beyond 65 years of age because they need to, in order to survive.

In the modern world, in even the wealthiest countries, this is generally what we have come to accept as normal. We may travel, we may have families, we may have barbeques or sip cocktails, but for the majority of people this is the life that we are familiar with and that we accept, whether we like it or not.

Yet for some people this is not the case. They have plenty of money and all the freedom and happiness in the world ... don't they? Don't they have the perfect lives that you read about in magazines? They can have *anything* they want ... can't they? This gives us more evidence that more money will make all our problems go away, giving us freedom and untold happiness.

But it's not true.

Looking from this perspective, however, it is easy to understand why we focus on money as the key to freedom and fulfilment: the more money you have, the less you need to work, and less work equals more freedom. We focus on the money thinking the freedom will come.

There are two problems with this focus. The first is the law of attraction. I won't go into this in depth because there are whole philosophies dedicated to it, but for the uninitiated, part of the law of attraction is that you get what you focus on whether it is positive or negative. For example, if your focus is on avoiding *not having enough money* then not enough money is what you'll get. Or, if we focus on not having enough time, not having enough time is what you'll get — make sense?

The second problem with a focus on money is that we are seldom satisfied. There seems to be a global condition that is simply not satisfied with enough or even with plenty; we strive to have the most, the biggest and the best. Companies are designed to make continual increasing profit for their shareholders and that is the bottom line. Despite their social responsibility efforts, behind the scenes all businesses must reduce costs and increase profits in order to survive and be seen as successful.

Regardless of your focus, as an employee you are likely to earn increasing amounts of money as you progress through your working life. Every time you change job, get promoted or take on more responsibility you are likely to earn more. But what happens to your lifestyle? As you are promoted you generally end up with more responsibility, more hours working and have less time to do the things you wanted the money for in the first place.

Your lifestyle will quickly grow to absorb your new funds. You will do more, have more expensive dinners, drive more expensive cars and buy more material possessions. Then you might have children and buy a house and you will need even more money to service your lifestyle. As you can see, the 'more money' lifestyle expands as quickly as you can earn more. Look at the wealthiest people in the world; notice that many people who are driven by money keep working for it, no matter how much they have. There is never enough for that insatiable more-money beast.

So how can you ignore money when it comes to creating your dream lifestyle? Well, the fact is, you can't. But, you can move the focus from making money and amassing great wealth to creating a fulfilling lifestyle that is funded by the things you are most passionate about, where you make enough money to give you the lifestyle you want.

What does your dream lifestyle look like?

Stop for a moment and imagine what your dream lifestyle looks like, and write it down.

➪ Where do you live?

➪ What passions are you exploring?

➪ What are you contributing to?

➪ What are you doing day to day?

My dream lifestyle...
1
2
etc.

As you go through your list, you may find that some of your aspirations are more achievable than you previously thought. How many of your goals are completely divorced from the need for more money?

Some people get to this point and notice that certain areas of their dream lifestyle are actually possible now, they just had been putting it off. If you are one of those people and you can see the actions you need to take to fulfil some of your lifestyle goals now then create some space in your diary to start those projects immediately! Whether it is teaching at an orphanage in Pakistan or singing in a band; create a plan now for it being a reality in the short term.

Like now. Yes, really … now.

My dream lifestyle involves living close to the beach in a warm climate; having plenty of time to play guitar and to cook each day, and share and enjoy meals with the people I love; sharing my ideas by writing blogs and books; participating in the work of charities and organisations focused on creating the basics of life as well as opportunities for disadvantaged children; using my businesses experience to coach small business owners and budding entrepreneurs and social entrepreneurs; and travelling the world freely to fall in love with new communities and cultures. My dream lifestyle allows me to work on things I enjoy, and not because I have to.

I am an ordinary 31-year-old woman living my dream life, and if I can do it, so can you.

Creating a good life crisis

We have all heard of a 'midlife crisis', but recently I heard the term a 'good life crisis'. This is a time in our lives when we are forced to reflect on our probable future (being much the same as it has already been), fuelling a compulsion to take action to create an alternative, something that opens the door to a good life. My good life crisis occurred in July 2006, following the success of a music festival I founded. This experience gave me a huge amount of self-confidence, and the next day I quit my job in the pursuit of business, lifestyle and adventure.

Looking back this was probably a little rash because I didn't know what I wanted to do and I hadn't set anything up for myself! But, I felt the undeniable urge to throw myself out of my comfort zone or I would lose another nine years thinking about it. I was naive, young and inexperienced, but I was going to give it my best shot. I often hear from business owners that they started their business as a result of unexpected events like a redundancy, being unable to find a job or a major health scare. These are people who are forced to look at how they are going to deal with life and realise that they have no time to lose.

I forced myself to take action by quitting my job and the comfortable income it provided. Others are forced to take action because of desperation or lack of other options. These are actually times when creating a new lifestyle seems less risky because you are already in a position of uncertainty—your motivation and need to succeed are piqued because it *has* to happen. While these are great motivators, it is trial by fire. What if you can create an easier transition?

The easy transition versus trial by fire

If you have a job that pays your bills and you have no financial urgency to create a new means of income then you have the opportunity to create an easier transition than the one that I created for myself! You have the opportunity to test your ideas and get started without the financial pressure that causes many good life crises.

What will make you successful in this scenario is the ability to emulate the mindset of urgency when there is no urgency, in creating haste without the madness of unexpected or difficult events.

To do this you need to be personally motivated. If you can muster the drive, you have a wonderful opportunity to create a smooth transition financially from your job to your new lifestyle business to provide you with income.

Starting this way can give you the space to get your head around the industry and your own new business without the pressure of needing to create an income from it immediately. Even if you don't have financial pressures spurring you on, it is important to have a schedule that you stick to as well as a revenue goal so that you know when you are ready and able to take the plunge (leave your day job or make your new business your main business).

It's never too late to start

What will be your good life crisis? What will it take for you to seriously start on the path to creating your dream lifestyle? Whether your drive is fuelled by dissatisfaction, desperation, passion, divine inspiration or just a desire to get more out of your existence, start now.

I spent nine years dissatisfied before I started on the path to follow my passions, and I am sure many of you have spent just as long, if not longer, dreaming of but postponing taking the action necessary to create your life of freedom and fulfilment.

What you will find on this journey is that some things will be easier than you think and some things will be harder than you think. The reality is that you won't know until you give it a go and there is no better time to start than now.

Take a moment to think about what a life worth living means to you. Think about what you really want from life. Make a list of the things that are really important to you and the things you want to achieve.

What is *really* important to me?
1
2
etc.

For me a life worth living means having the freedom to spend my time doing things I am really interested in, which include my family, writing, cooking, playing music, travelling and helping people see what is possible for their lives despite their current circumstances.

As you can see, none of the things that make my life worth living have anything to do with money.

I realised that there isn't any red pill, or even if there is, it wasn't going to be handed to me on a platter, so after years of chasing the illusive first million I dreamed of as a teenager, it became clear to me that I am not motivated by money. Let me say that again: *I am not motivated by money.* I certainly would get excited at the prospect of having millions of dollars and the opportunities that would provide, but I am not motivated by it.

The truth is, money makes no difference to our levels of happiness and fulfilment. The only caveat here are those who do not have enough for the basics of life, in which case money can make a huge difference to one's ability to live. Regardless of your situation in life, money will not satisfy any of your deeper and emotional needs and will not increase your general happiness. Happiness comes from other sources, and despite most of us knowing this we still cling to the hope of making millions and many of our goals in life remain financially driven.

This brings me to ask you to consider what your life would be like if you stopped participating in the rat race, swapping your money-oriented goals for all the things you wrote above —the things that are really important to you. If the nature of your work allowed you geographic freedom (you could work from anywhere) and you were doing something you thoroughly enjoyed, would you want to live in the same place and spend your time doing the things that you do now?

What lights your fire?

What excites you and puts the shimmy in your step time and time again?

When choosing a lifestyle business goal, it is essential to choose something that is a big enough motivator to get you out of bed each day and keep you going when it gets hard. It needs to be something that really lights your fire!

If your business goal does not thrill the pants off you, it will quickly add to your pile of other goals that didn't really do it for you. You know those things you wanted to achieve, that you never quite finished (or even started)?

This includes money goals. If your goal is simply to make lots of money, you may find that it isn't a big enough motivator for success. Think how many people have started multi-level-marketing schemes with dreams of large incomes, only to find that they are not motivated enough to do the work. I recently heard the statistics from a well-established multi-level-marketing scheme and was not surprised to hear that less than 5 per cent of people who joined created any sort of regular income. Worse still, they estimated that less than 1 per cent of people who joined could be considered financially viable as a result.

What I suggest is that if you think that making lots of money is your big amazing goal, dig a little deeper. For example, think about what you would do with the money if you had it. What adventures would you have? Who would you help? What experiences would you create? Your answers will give you a goal far more inspiring than a quest for cash.

Look back at the dream lifestyle list you made and cross out any money-oriented goals. Now, think about what else you can come up with if you were to pursue only what you are really passionate about.

By making passion and lifestyle our driver rather than a need for money, we start to alter how we think and operate. You may have already started choosing projects and directions that really inspire you. From my experience (and that of the many people I have worked with), when we do this we start to get genuinely excited about life. We increase the level of attention we give to the details and become very interested in doing the best job possible to achieve our goals. Add to this the sense of fulfilment that accompanies the successes and your mindset starts to change significantly.

This does not mean you should carelessly abandon all concerns about money. We all have needs which must be looked after, but it is possible to meet our financial responsibilities while living lives that fulfil our passions as well. Finding an incentive and lifestyle goal worth having, and feeling confident enough to chase it, will open doors to living your dream lifestyle sooner rather than later. It really is the opportunity to have it all.

Your inherent value

Later in the book we will look at how you can create value from your passions and experiences through your own internet business. But before we delve into the technical steps, I want to talk about how valuable *you* are.

Value is subjective and every person you meet and every situation you find yourself in will come with a different measure of value. In any given day, your perceived value will waver as a result of the interactions you have with people or as a result of your achievements. For example, if you can't help someone with directions you have low value as a guide, but if you help your colleague find a contact lens in the carpet you have high value as an extra pair of eyes. If you burn the risotto you have low value as a chef, but if you are outgoing, bubbly and fun you have high value in social situations.

In some areas of life our value is easily measured. For example, salespeople know their financial contribution to a company's revenue stream, and a parent would know that their children are fed, clothed and happy. But more often than not our value comes down to opinion and your measure of your own self-worth.

Often our value is arbitrarily judged by our income or job description, and this is an area where things can get a little sticky. The problem with using your job as a measure for value is that you might lose your job one day, or be unhappy and want to leave. If you suddenly have no job, does this mean that you have no value? Of course not! But this is how many people operate. I have seen many brilliant people fall into this trap. More often than not they are unaware of how much they relied on their job and income as a measure of their value until they suddenly found themselves without it.

If you think that you might subscribe to the same value judgement habit (and I believe that many people do), start looking within for a more authentic judgement of your value. This is essential if you are considering business because if you start a business when you have a low opinion of your self-worth, your business will reflect this and you will undervalue your business and services. This would not be a good start on the path to your sustainable low-maintenance income!

Generating and sustaining your perception of value

If you are serious about creating a successful business opportunity, as well as the technical aspects of your business you need to consider the fact that there will be a period of work before you are successful. Can you sustain your value during the time before you produce results? Can you maintain your feeling of value even if things don't go as planned if it takes longer than you had anticipated?

Being able to generate your own measure of value, separate from your results, is a trait that will make creating your business opportunities and dream lifestyle goals easier and a lot more fun. It will also smooth over some of the difficulties and failures you are bound to experience. Yes, you will fail at some things, and no, this does not make you a failure!

If you start to recognise that your level of personal value directly correlates to your success or failure on every part of the journey, consider your personal development equally as important as your business development. Increasing your perception of your own value comes from personal growth and achievement.

There are thousands of books, courses and adventures you can have that will help you on this path. Grab every opportunity to challenge the way you perceive yourself as you embark on your business journey. Not only will this give your business a greater chance of success, you will probably find a new level of general happiness and perspective, and that can't be a bad thing!

You are a walking, talking, value-making machine

Once you have your vision for your dream lifestyle and your measure of personal value in check, it is time to look at what value you have to offer in the way of skills, experiences, opinions and entertainment. This is the foundation for your income-generating opportunities; this is the bit where you get to let your creativity, passion and knowledge run amok.

The style of business I will share with you in this book is about creating a community on the internet. You will create a community of like-minded people with similar interests, experiences or values. I will show that you can create value for this community and make a contribution. In return, you will have the ability to create alternative sources of income.

Imagine how fulfilling your life will be when you are able to share what's in your head and have it contribute to others 24 hours a day, 365 days a year, even when you are sleeping.

You have a lifetime of experiences, skills, knowledge and passions that are unlike any person who has ever lived. No-one has the exact same perspective, knowledge or experience as you, which provides a unique grab-bag from which you can pick and share with others.

You will have hundreds, if not thousands, of things that you can share that would be of value to other people in this world that would come from jobs you have worked, experiences you have had, people you have met and things you have observed. Things like how to grow indoor herbs, cook for children with allergies, soothe broken hearts, live with a chronic illness or spot antique treasures at garage sales. You might know how to design websites, fix old doors, sizzle the perfect sausage or make origami animals. The list goes on and on and on.

Sharing any of these (and countless other) skills, knowledge and experiences would be useful to someone finding themselves with the same situation or questions you had, wanting to know more or learn the skills you have developed.

The internet is an ever-increasing source of weird and wonderful information, and for the most part much of what we want to know, do or experience will be documented in some form if you look hard enough.

Even if a website exists that covers your area of skill, knowledge or experience there is always room for more—so don't worry if you find other websites covering what you know, can do or have experience with. We often look at several websites on a similar topic, because we are looking for a particular type of information or want to verify the accuracy of information through corroboration from several sources. As consumers we prefer there to be several websites on a topic, which means as a website owner there is always room for one more.

 Case study: Grassroots Internet Strategy

As a business coach I help small business owners plan for success by overcoming any challenges they face along the way. Over the years I recognised that a large percentage of small business owners suffer the same problem; they build websites that do not give them the results they want or need to grow their business. They are disappointed with the traffic, the income or sales leads it generates, or they are just not able to update it easily. All of these outcomes can mean the difference between success and failure in a fledgling small business, and I see many people struggle.

The causes of these problems vary greatly, but most of them could have been avoided if the business owner had learned the basic principles of creating a successful website before starting out.

The worst thing is that by the time people come to me, they have already spent a lot of time and money on their website and in some cases they need to start again from scratch.

I empathise with them as my first business crumbled for the same reason. In my first business I lacked the knowledge I needed to plan for, produce and market a website that would generate income. The real problem for me was that I had no idea what I needed to learn. This cost me the business.

There is nothing like failure to drive you to succeed! I wanted to learn everything I could about how to have a successful website. Several years and lots of experience and learning later, I now support people with exactly the same problems I experienced.

I saw an opportunity to create a website that would help business owners with all of the fundamentals to create a successful website, a website that simplified the industry and the jargon, that was easily accessible for small business owners with lots of step-by-step information.

I had found an area where I could apply my knowledge and experience to contribute significantly to helping business owners avoid many of the common problems that they would face. I found a way to *give value*.

You do not need to be an expert to be of value

The internet is very generous to website owners and bloggers. You can be completely open and honest on the internet as an amateur enthusiast and that is enough to create an interested community if they appreciate what you share and how you share it. You do not have to be a seasoned expert on a subject with a PhD or need 10 years' experience to be of value to your community. You simply need to be passionate about exploring the industry and sharing what you know and discover.

For example, if you are a mother who has a child with an allergy to peanuts, your experience in dealing with the emotional side of looking after your child and finding appropriate foods, coupled with your collection of recipes and tips, can be enough to start a community.

If you are a person who has been through a major health scare, your witty, heartfelt or matter-of-fact observations or tips on life and death, emotions, hospitals and illness can similarly be enough to start a community.

We are far more likely to trust the opinions of our peers than of external influencers, and the internet gives you an opportunity to create a community of like-minded people with whom you can share an experience and develop trust. If you have provided good tips on car maintenance that have worked for me in the past, I might trust your opinion above my new mechanic. If you have suggested a great jeweller and I have found we share the same taste, I would be inclined to believe your opinion rather than that of an advert on television.

Internet communities are built on common interest and trust, which you gain by generously sharing what you know or have experienced.

Keep in mind that sometimes it can be much more interesting to follow a journey of exploration from the outset rather than to hear from the victor at the end. When sharing about the past, details can be exaggerated, forgotten, generalised, glossed over, and stories become more about what you want to remember than the facts. If, however, you witness a journey from the outset, you get to really be part of the journey and follow a real person, witnessing the experience as it unfolds.

Whether or not you are a trained expert, your ability to attract an audience and have people keep coming back is based on your ability to provide *value,* and that is the foundation upon which this book is established.

It does not matter how niche your knowledge is, you can create value from it. The beautiful thing about the opportunity before you is that even if there are only 5000 interested people in the whole world, through the internet it is possible for you to connect with them.

The internet is packed full of websites that are solely based on the specific knowledge and experiences of their owners. For example, Belle Gurd and Nicolas Brown set up their Moving 2 London website once they saw that they could share their experiences of what they were learning the hard way. After moving to London they realised that there was no one-stop-shop for all the information they needed to settle comfortably there.

They decided to collate everything useful they found so that others could benefit. Were they experts on London? Not at first, but they made it their mission to look for every possible piece of information that would benefit those who migrated there. In doing so they created an experience-based resource that helps thousands of people a year who are reading their website and buying their comprehensive moving guide.

Always be honest and transparent

When sharing your experiences your intention is for people to consume your work! So, make sure you are responsible and do not mislead people or make statements that could be misconstrued as fact. Especially in industries such as health and the law, for example, be very sure that you do not come across as a qualified expert if you are not one. You want to build trust with your community, and misleading people is not a good way to do that—even inadvertently!

Using what's in your head to create an income

Like everybody, your passions, skills and life experiences and the way that you have dealt with them provide you with a wealth of responses to other people's questions, problems, wants and needs. Your ability to create an income from your pre-existing knowledge will not depend on whether you have anything to offer, but on your ability to:

☞ package your skills, knowledge and experience accessibly and attractively

☞ ensure your offerings are found by the people who want and need them

☞ practise the fundamentals of generating revenue online.

Every topic that you have knowledge or opinions about could be of value to people interested in the same topic. You are a walking, talking library of potential assistance, inspiration or entertainment, much of which, if packaged and presented attractively and marketed well, can create an income for you.

Here are some examples of people who have used their experience and passions to assist or entertain others on the internet and which they are using as the foundation for creating income.

Charlotte Squire spreads a message of positivity, happiness and environmental sustainability through her positive news website Happyzine. She creates value by collating articles and inspiring writers to contribute to her weekly blog. Her e-zine is read by thousands of people, and she provides positive writing courses as well as a funky eBook teaching people *Ten Ways to Have Fun and Chillax as You Live Your Green Dreams.*

When Katrina Musgrave found that it was hard to know when and where children's markets were scheduled, she developed her Market Angel website that shares local insight, as well as a national directory of markets that is of value to both the stall holders and potential visitors.

When Pat Flynn was unexpectedly made redundant he taught himself how to make an income online and shares his knowledge on The Smart Passive Income Blog. He has created a massive community of people who appreciate his honest and comprehensive sharing of everything he discovers along the way.

As you can see these are not necessarily specialists or experts, they are simply motivated people who found a way to create value from something they enjoy and market it on online.

What have you got to share?

Now it's your turn. Start to think about what you have to share —think about how you could inform, inspire or entertain. List in your notebook 10 topics you have knowledge about.

To get you started, think back through your life: what experiences challenged you? What did you learn that made life easier, better or different? What do you think, read or talk about that would be of interest to other people? What skills do you have that you could share with others?

To give you some examples, here is the list I wrote:

1 I have experience in organising and running music and fundraising events.

2 People seek me out for advice on relationships and dealing with life's ups and downs.

3 I really enjoy talking about music, bands and festivals.

4 I know how to host a radio show.

5 I love to help people with small business start-up or expansion.

6 I have a passion for healthy and delicious food.

7 I know lots of effective techniques to assist people to market their business on the internet.

8 I am really good at connecting people with skills with people who need them.

9 I can assist people to understand how to use the internet to create a low-maintenance income.

10 I have strong views about how humans should treat each other, animals and the environment.

Now write yours:

What have I got to share?
1
2
etc.

With this list you will see that you already have at least 10 topics which could be of value to people on the internet. Every one of the things you have listed here is a potential starting point for a website business.

 Case study: Grassroots Internet Strategy

For Grassroots Internet Strategy the topic seemed to choose me. It was the thing that most people were asking me about, and it was something that I loved to share. One day on Facebook I saw that an ex-colleague Melinda Samson had started a business in website copywriting and search engine marketing. Her skills were perfectly complementary to mine in solving lots of the problems people were asking about. Similarly, her clients were asking the same questions and were coming to her to fix the same problems with their websites; *we had identified a need.*

We decided to create a website together where we would help others with the same advice and hopefully make it more accessible *before* business owners spent sometimes thousands of dollars or hundreds of hours on their websites.

We both had a good level of knowledge about certain areas of internet marketing, having each been responsible for the production of websites within both corporate and small business worlds. While we had experience in many aspects of internet marketing, we did not have any experience in producing this type of website. In addition, we had a very small budget to work with so we had to be creative.

What we did have, however, was a huge commitment that the business would succeed and we were both passionate about the outcome and how beneficial it would be to others. We gave ourselves 12 months to set up the business, and have at least three information products available to generate income. I am certain that our passion, commitment and willingness were the key ingredients that ensured we were successful in achieving our goal!

The wrap-up

The first step in achieving your dream lifestyle is being clear on what that lifestyle is and what you really want from life. Think about the following:

- Understand why money is the wrong goal. If you remove all money goals, what are you left with? Is it possible to achieve some of those goals now?

- What constitutes your dream lifestyle? Create a clear picture of what it is you are aiming for.

- What will be the catalyst for your good life crisis? Find something important enough to motivate you to succeed (without the need for an actual crisis!).

- It is really never too late to start, and there is no time to waste! Find a lifestyle business that really lights your fire.

- It is important to develop personally as you embark on a business adventure because your perception of your own value will carry over into your business. Remember to tie in personal development as well as business development.

✏️ You are a walking, talking, value-making machine. Your experiences, skills and opinions are all possible areas in which you can share and create value on the internet, even if someone else is already doing it.

✏️ The internet is generous: you can create as much value for people as a complete amateur as you can with 20 years' experience.

The success mindset

In this chapter we will look at some elements for success that I have found to be critical on the journey to creating a low-maintenance income. None of them relate to knowledge, skill or experience, and they have everything to do with your attitude and approach. Like any pursuit or challenge in life, your mindset will be the determining factor in your success.

Being able to recognise your mindset traits and develop ones that empower you is a powerful skill. It comes naturally for some people and others need to develop the skill, but I believe that everyone has the capacity to do this. Your brain is incredibly powerful, and, as you probably know, we only use a small percentage of its capabilities. As well as the benefits of fitness, healthy eating and plenty of laughter, these mindset tips form the philosophy by which I live, work and play.

Analysis paralysis

'Action will remove the doubts that theory cannot solve.'
Tehyi Hsieh

If you have ever let a fear of the unknown stop you from doing something you really wanted to do or grabbing a great opportunity, you have probably suffered from analysis paralysis. Those who suffer from analysis paralysis can spend months (or years) procrastinating over decisions, especially when starting projects that could be challenging or life changing. It is a crippling condition because it gives sufferers an unlimited supply of excuses for not taking action through excessive analysis of the situation, such as: 'It is not the right time'. The problem is that these excuses can seem extremely valid. If you look hard enough you can always find an excuse not to proceed.

This over-analysis and procrastination is not to be confused with careful planning; some projects require us to consider timing or to gain experience so we can make the most of an opportunity. So, how do you distinguish careful planning from analysis paralysis? People who are genuinely planning their project are taking *action*: they have started, they are doing their research, plotting their course, talking to people and taking action. People suffering from analysis paralysis, however, are just *thinking* about the best course of action: they may be dreaming or talking but they are not actually doing anything.

Every success you will have in life will be as a result of taking action. If you ask the most successful people in any field you will see one common thread: they had a vision and they took action to achieve it. They realised that failure was possible yet they took action anyway. They realised that you do not need to know how to succeed; you just need to be willing to start and know that getting it wrong or failing are part of the process of learning how to succeed.

Imagine if we never learned to drive, handle money or interview for a job, or never left home to explore the world because we did not know how or were scared that we may not get it right. The world would be very different! This is the kind of attitude that many bring to discovering how to make their dreams come true. With this mindset you will not realise your dreams or live the life you really want to live.

Mahatma Gandhi once said that 'you may never know what results come of your actions, but if you do nothing, there will be no results'. If you find yourself procrastinating with concerns like *I don't know what to do*, *I don't have the right tools*, *am I doing it correctly*, *do I know enough* or *am I the right person*, you are probably suffering from analysis paralysis and things will happen very slowly — or not at all.

How to eliminate analysis paralysis

Taking the first step is what differentiates people who achieve big goals and people who do not. Your thoughts and dreams can only become real when you set yourself goals with time frames and take action towards achieving them. Define your goal with a 'what by when' and then share it with the people around you. For example, some 'what by when' goals I created were:

What?	By when?
1 Stage a concert featuring five bands to promote racial harmony	July 2006
2 Start a coaching business to help small business owners	September 2008
3 Create a low-maintenance income and record the whole process	December 2010

Have a go. Write down five of your goals, and next to them insert a date by when you want to realise them.

Real fear versus chemical trickery

Analysis paralysis stops you taking action, and in my experience is usually a reaction to one or more of the following fears — the fear of:

➪ failure

⮞ success

⮞ feeling or looking incompetent or inadequate

⮞ being rejected or feeling unloved

⮞ making the wrong choices

⮞ not getting the outcome you want

⮞ not knowing what to do or how to do it.

The reason these fears seem so real is that our bodies tell us they are! Our brains trick us into believing that these situations are comparable to real physical dangers. This is because the same chemicals are released from our brains when our lives are threatened by a gun-wielding maniac as when we are standing in front of an auditorium full of people waiting for us to speak. Fear is a chain reaction in the brain that starts with a stressful stimulus and ends with a release of chemicals that causes, among other things, a racing heart, fast breathing and energised muscles.

When considering the start of your dream project, some of the fears listed above can create heart palpitations, panic and sweats in the same way as if you were in physical danger. When a project is large or challenging, I will often experience moments of fear as to whether I will pull it off. I find that the more important the project is to me, the more my body tests my resolve with surges of chemical trickery.

You would have noticed a similar chemical rush in times when you have been afraid. If you have ever pushed yourself out of your comfort zone by doing things like bungee jumping, parachuting, speaking in front of a large group of people or confronting a friend, more than likely you would have experienced some level of fear or nerves. However, although you were scared at the thought of doing those things, you did them anyway and lived to tell the tale ... but do we learn from this? No! We continue to let fear stop us in many other circumstances — including when we want to chase our dreams.

It is sad to see so many people missing out on the things they really want in life because of this. However, fear not! It is possible to put fear in perspective.

Putting fear into perspective

One autumn afternoon I was swimming at a beach which is known for strong currents. On this day it was particularly rough and choppy. Although I am not a bad swimmer, I prefer calm seas, and to avoid the waves I usually swim out past the breakers to deeper water.

On this day, however, there had been a storm and I spent a long time navigating crashing waves and strong, multi-directional currents. Suddenly I realised that I was being dragged out to the side of the beach towards another bay, but, more worryingly, also towards some jagged rocks looming in between.

Adrenalin kicked in as I tried to swim sideways out of the current, but no luck. I was being dragged backwards faster than I could swim. I looked out at the lifeguard station and it seemed very far away. My immediate fear was being smashed onto the rocks, but my focus quickly shifted to the speed and power with which the next set of waves pounded me. I dived through, gasped, and dived through the next one, but it was too late. The world was spinning, with water and sand swirling everywhere. I got my bearings and then opened my eyes just long enough to see the next wave breaking above me before I tumbled again.

Luckily a passing knight had noticed my predicament and was able to pull me to shore, shaken and tired but unhurt. As I recovered on the sand, it occurred to me how infrequently I encounter genuinely dangerous situations and how lucky that makes me. I realised that the fear I feel in my day-to-day living is a luxury compared to millions of people around the world whose daily fears come from real dangers like being maimed or killed in warfare, starving to death, not being able to get medical care for sick family members or being homeless. If my physical experience of fear in a life-threatening situation was the same physical experience I had when I was not in a life-threatening situation, perhaps I was overreacting to many of the daily risks and challenges I faced.

While lying there in the sand I decided that when I face the normal situations that cause me fear—such as when I speak in public—I would remember this experience and use it as a measure of danger. I would allow myself to feel fear only if I was in real danger. No danger meant I needed to take a deep breath and harden up!

Now it's your turn

Now it's your turn to put fear into perspective so you can recognise the chemical trickery that will stop you in your tracks. If you find that fear stops you from doing what you want to do, compare it to the last time you were genuinely in physical danger. Think back to what happened. Take yourself through the experience in your mind. Maybe you had a car accident, slipped and fell or got lost while hiking. Think about how you felt, the physical sensations and all the emotions. Now that is fear based on real danger. Anything else is your mind giving you a dose of chemical trickery.

If you can't remember any particular experience, you can create one! Try a new extreme sport, jump on a massive rollercoaster, go skydiving...just do something that will make you scream.

When you are moving through your journey to create your dream lifestyle and you start to find you are stopped by fear, take yourself back to an experience of 'real fear' and use that as a barometer for your mental fear, and then...have a laugh at yourself and carry on.

Act like anything is possible...because it is!

What separates where you are right now and where you want to be is a series of actions. Every goal you have is achievable by fulfilling all of the actions necessary to reach the goal. What is critical is the mindset you bring to the situation. If you approach a project or goal with a series of concerns about how big and difficult it is and how you are likely to fail, the chances are that you will prove yourself right and you probably won't succeed. But if you approach it with the mindset that anything is possible, the chances of you achieving your goal are already greatly increased—believe me, I know!

 Case study: act like anything is possible

A few years ago I decided to stage a concert because I wanted to encourage racial harmony in my local area. I had no idea how to do it, very little spare time in which to organise it and no finances with which to set it up. It was not an industry that I knew anything about and I had no idea who could help me. I knew I needed a venue, bands and a crowd, but that was about it! As you can see I had plenty of reasons to plonk down in front of the TV and forget about the whole thing ... but I was determined that anything was possible and I was going to hold a concert!

For an event this size I wanted to work with a team—a team passionate about music and racial harmony, and who would have some skills that I did not have. So, looking for people to join my team to make the event happen, I started to tell everyone I knew about the plan for the concert, looking to fill all the gaps. A few weeks in I met Alex and Gordon, who also became excited about what was possible—and who also had no idea how to stage a concert of this size. There we were: three idealistic, passionate people, with very little experience in running big music concerts.

Sometimes the required actions are not clear straight away, and in these instances all you can do is take the actions you know to take. At a basic level I knew that I needed a venue, bands and a crowd. Every conversation I had with people expanded the idea and opportunities further while making it clearer what we needed to do. By talking to more and more people, I was inadvertently making the concert more real; it started to take on a life and form

Case study *(cont'd)*: act like anything is possible

of its own, and soon the event was becoming much bigger than my original dreams for it. There was now an expectation that I was going to put on a show, and there was no room for me to stop, procrastinate or get an attack of analysis paralysis.

I rang the manager of the local radio station to seek advice about how to approach radio stations to help with marketing. Instead of just giving me his advice, he said he wanted to broadcast the event live on the radio. Similarly, when I contacted the venue I wanted to use and told them of my plan for five bands, they offered to help by providing four stages and a budget for twenty bands. My concert turned into a festival in two conversations!

After six weeks of outrageous action there was a core team of seven people, sponsors for a venue, 20 bands, staging and marketing, partnership from the local radio station, a compilation album underway and a feeling that anything really is possible. We even started to aim for 1500 people to come to the festival.

On 30 July 2006 we had the chance to find out if our work had paid off—and we were dazzled with the day of all days! The bands played their hearts out, the people danced and sang and shared the love, the venue had experienced its biggest day ever, and by the time the last band on the last stage finished and the calls for encores subsided over 8000 people had come through the doors.

Holding this event made me realise that each time I took a positive action, made a phone call or invited someone to participate, opportunities far greater and more interesting than my original goal opened up. But, I would never have known if I had not taken action and called the people who I thought may be able to help or want to get involved.

For the first time in my life, I was genuinely acting on every one of the 'should do's' that were on my list, and the experience was magic. I was completely open to creating something huge and I was unstoppable in finding what we needed to make it work. It's an incredible way to spend life that generates an enormous amount of positive energy.

If I look back and analyse the source of the magic, I can see that we had the attitude that we would seize the day and take action. We acted like anything is possible, and for the first time in our lives we found all the evidence we needed to believe it.

As a result of the festival's success and my (then) newfound mindset that anything is possible, I resigned the next day from my job and career to pursue my passions. I look back on this time and see that I was probably running nearly entirely with the mindset that anything is possible, and for this reason, it was. I had no idea how to make it work, so my only tool was to take every action I thought to take at the time.

The pitfall is that if I don't keep fresh and take these types of actions all the time, I will fall back into mindsets of what is logical and 'possible', and the results of those actions are more logical and realistic...*boring*! To combat this I am constantly searching for new challenges that require me to refresh the notion that anything is possible if you take the actions needed to achieve it.

Be persistent

Being persistent and unstoppable is an essential trait for success in life. Regardless of your skill, experience, intelligence or fabulous good looks, unless you are willing to persist with what you are committed to you will struggle to achieve many of the things that are available to you.

Sure, there are some great things that you can have given to you on a plate, but on the whole most of the things that are really worth having require some commitment and effort to achieve or maintain. Even with just a quick look at my life, I can safely say that my persistence and determination have been the foundation for the majority of the amazing experiences, discoveries and love that I now enjoy.

Persistence is what has driven me through the hard times, particularly when my first business was failing. The challenges I navigated during this period were the turning point in my life. With every failure, I experienced being one step closer to achieving the vision that I have for my life, at times stripped of everything but sheer determination.

Now, when coaching small business owners I can give real examples of what does and does not work, more often than not because I have tried it. I live by Sir Thomas Edison's maxim when inventing the light bulb: 'I have not failed. I've just found 10 000 ways that won't work.'

It is the juice of the challenging, sometimes seemingly impossible situations that have made me understand what it is to be flailing in the swamp of failure, to grit my teeth and emerge on the other side, into an incredible land where anything is possible. This is something only the persistent get to experience.

The key to persistence

The key to persistence is a simple two-word question, the answer to which will provide everything you need on your journey to great adventure and fulfilment. The question is: *what's next?* This is how it works. Look at your current situation and just ask yourself... what's next?

You are one step closer to your goal... what's next?

You feel like you have done everything you can and you are about to fail... what's next?

You don't know what to do... what's next?

You are overwhelmed and it is all too much... what's next?

By asking yourself what's next and having the courage to answer the question and take the actions necessary, you have the key that unlocks your universe as powerfully as asking 'why?' when you were three years old. Asking 'what's next' acknowledges that there is always something more, that there is always another step that you can take if you choose to.

The relationship between persistence and luck

You create your own luck, and there is a very close relationship between persistence and luck, as exemplified by my little brother Sam. One of my vivid childhood memories is of walking down the street in a small town in New Zealand with Sam. I was about 10 (he 8) and we were sauntering along when Sam bent over and picked up a $20 note out of the gutter. When you are a kid in New Zealand in the 1980s $20 is a lot of money. My brother was notoriously lucky at finding money — 50¢ here or $2 there…lucky, lucky Sam would always find money! So while this was an especially large find, the find itself was not unusual.

Sam taught me my first real lesson in luck, and more importantly that you create your own luck. This was because on any given day if you followed my brother down the road, you would see a little boy on the hunt, kicking aside leaves, flipping over stones, testing parking meters, scrounging in bins, emptying bags and peering over walls, always with his eyes peeled, always looking for money.

While it might sound like he was a young hobo, he was simply dedicated in his pursuit of an increase in his personal wealth. People from the outside only saw how lucky he was, but the secret to his so-called luck was determination and persistence — he was a boy out to create his own luck, and as he matured, so did his opportunities.

From the outside any achievement may seem lucky, because you haven't seen the months or years of dedication that went into it — don't be fooled! Be persistent in your endeavours, act like anything is possible and you will find so-called lucky breaks seem to happen more and more frequently.

Selective hearing

Even the most persistent among us can get thrown off course by negative opinions, judgements and assessments about what we are doing. Every person you come into contact with (and some you will never meet) will have a view about who you are, what you are doing and what you should do. This can be disheartening, especially if you are feeling vulnerable when, for example, your dream project is struggling to work or you are trying something new, big and scary. To deal with this positively, you need to develop selective hearing. Selective hearing enables you to listen to people who support you or who have good ideas and present new opportunities, while you smile and filter out all the people who try to dissuade you or dampen your enthusiasm.

It may take some time to develop the skill of avoiding the 'noise'. First you need to realise and accept that some people who you think *should* support you and who you *want* to support you will not. This might be difficult to deal with, but remember that some of the people closest to you will feel like it is their duty to protect you from harm, and these people may not be operating from the same sense that *anything is possible* and therefore might not see that your goals are achievable. Add to that the possibility that they may be suffering from their own form of analysis paralysis and it is no surprise that you may be steered back onto a more logical and reasonable course with all the best intentions.

This is part of a conversation I had with a well-meaning person in my life:

'Serena, you shouldn't quit your job. It's a good job with good money.'

'But it's not what I want to do; I want to try my hand at a fulfilling business.'

'But it's a *good job*. You are *crazy* to quit!'

I have found that the more outrageous the goal, the louder the noise. It's natural for people to have an opinion, and the more you give them to think about, the more of an opinion they will have. I now accept that some people I know and love do not understand, agree with or care about what I am doing and that is just part of the adventure.

How you can develop selective hearing

Find a few people who understand your project, business or vision, who have your success at heart and with whom you can create an environment where they can support you. This could include mentors and a coach as well as personal confidants. This will give you a base of support so that you have confidence when you put yourself out in the world. Speak to your support people on a regular basis and give yourself permission to smile, and politely ignore the words from anyone else who doesn't understand or support you in achieving your dreams.

Failure is a step on the path to success

'Success is the ability to go from failure to failure without losing your enthusiasm.'
Sir Winston Churchill

You *are* going to fail at some things. It is absolutely, positively going to happen. If you can find me a person who has succeeded at every single thing they put their mind to, I will bring you a goose that lays golden eggs. Everyone fails at some time. And here is the bad news—the more goals you create and the more risks you take, the more things you will potentially fail at.

So ... what's next?

I have failed many times. In all sorts of things ... so many things! In this book I have mentioned a selection of times where I learned a lesson in life or business. But I could fill another whole book with all of the other things I tried, many that succeeded and many that failed, as any successful person could. If you are really looking for the juice of life, you need to have an attitude that embraces failure, because it means that you are brave enough to take risks in pursuit of having the things that are important to you.

Failure is one of the risks of being entrepreneurial, and it is for this reason that we celebrate the successes. Don't be fooled though, we usually only become aware of someone's work when they become successful; we seldom see the journey from the outset, the previous failures, the hard work or struggle before someone hits the big time.

Failure is commonplace in business and I see many emotional decisions made because people resist failing like it is akin to death. They add a level of stress, anxiety and panic which over time is detrimental to the business and will potentially kill it. The unfortunate thing is that many people have to fail massively before they relax and realise that life will go on long after the disappointment of any failure wears off, and that there will always be plenty more opportunities for success.

Take on failure as an art form, because every failure you experience is a step on the path to your success. If you use failure as a time for reflection and growth, you will benefit from every setback and ultimately these will add to the stories you tell when you write a book and share the keys to your success!

Turning failure into growth

Try this two-step process for dealing with failure:

➥ *Be calm and reflect.* With each setback you encounter, take some time to calmly reflect on what you could have done differently. Consider what you are responsible for. If you are blaming someone else then you are too emotionally involved. Look for what *you* could have done that would have changed the outcome. Spend some time thinking about this and be creative with possible alternatives. If you are open to this exercise, you may notice some habits you possess that were not helpful for the outcome you were trying to achieve.

➥ *Create the lesson.* Once you are clear on how you could have changed the outcome, create the lesson that you will take from the experience. This is your opportunity to learn and grow; the lesson can be anything that will give you confidence that you can do better next time and it will motivate you to start again.

Some of the lessons I have taken from some of my failures are:

➭ *Work on the important stuff first.* In this failure I realised that I got too wrapped up in the minutiae of certain things instead of prioritising my time based on the crucial things. The lesson was to stop every once in a while and review where I am spending my time.

➭ *Don't take any more rubbish!* In this failure I realised that I was letting people do and say things that were either taking advantage or emotionally bullying. The lesson was to stand up for myself and not tolerate that kind of behaviour.

➭ *Get an outside perspective.* In this failure I felt like I was stuck and had no idea what I could do to improve the situation. The lesson was to go through the whole operation with an external person (a coach) from time to time to see what they could find missing in my approach.

Every failure you encounter will suggest that you stepped out of your comfort zone; this is something to be celebrated, and as ever it is time to ask yourself that magic question … what's next?

Be generous

Your lifestyle business will be built on a foundation of the energy that you inject into it, and there is no more positive energy than what is created with generosity.

Generosity is providing something to someone without expecting anything in return. The great thing about generosity is that it is free, there is no right or wrong or measure of it and it takes the focus away from our own crazy thoughts for at least a few moments! Whether it is your clients, friends, partner, family, a salesperson on the phone or a complete stranger, when it comes to generosity we have two Shakespearean choices … to be, or not to be.

Generosity is a warm smile to a complete stranger, holding someone in high esteem when they are down on themselves, or sharing your expertise and knowledge with someone who needs it. It is helping someone solve a problem or being patient when dealing with difficult people.

We often have the opportunity to be generous with people we are close to. Sometimes all it takes to refresh or transform a relationship is a few moments each day to acknowledge or understand your loved ones.

Generosity is a two-way street. It is equally important to allow others to be generous towards you. If you find yourself denying others attempts to be generous—stop it. Let it in; accept the generosity with humility and appreciation. You will find in a very short time that you are cultivating better relationships with friends and colleagues, and in my experience it provides the foundation for the best life partnerships imaginable!

In our high-speed world where there are so many automated and faceless transactions you can never be too generous, and with the bonus of the energy you create around you it is worthwhile getting in the habit for the start of your new business adventure.

Trust your intuition

Intuition, also known as your gut feeling, is when you experience an inexplicable urge to do, not do, agree or disagree with something. It gives you a feeling but it is not a feeling. It is a knowing without knowing. It means everything and nothing. It is a judgement without emotion. We are all gifted with intuition, but the extent to which we use it depends upon the extent to which we are aware of it. Some of us 'tune in' regularly and others have fleeting and occasional moments of clarity or certainty, but few of us really harness its potential to guide us.

I only became aware of my intuition a few years ago, after participating in some personal development courses and paying more attention to what was going on around me. I found that my willingness and ability to listen to and trust my intuition came hand in hand with my sense of inner peace, personal growth and happiness.

When I analyse this and break it down, I realise that trusting my instincts has directed me through many of the challenges in my life. I can relate most of my moments or periods of stupidity to when I didn't trust my gut instinct and went with an option that seemed easier or more logical.

Three ways to develop your intuition

Here are some ideas for how you can develop your intuition.

Ask yourself 'what is my gut telling me?'

This question, as simple as it sounds, is usually answered by your intuition. I ask it all the time of people who are struggling with decisions; and the answer is always there, yet often clouded with arguments, logic and fear.

If you are at any crossroads in decision-making, ask yourself 'what is my gut telling me?', and then acknowledge the answer. Good practice for this is asking other people who are struggling with a decision. You get to see intuition at work and it is great to watch! If asked, people will answer immediately with their instinct, then add reason and logic afterwards. Recognising that we do this and distinguishing the reason and logic are important steps in learning how to untangle our instincts from reason and logic and ultimately to trusting our gut.

Get in the habit of asking this question every time a decision needs to be made, regardless of what decision you eventually make. It is important to notice what your instinct was in the first place.

Develop listening *rather than* hearing

Listening is something that we vastly underuse! Do you listen for the communication being delivered or do you hear what is being said? There is a *big* difference. Many millions of communications each day are misconstrued because we are hearing the words but we are missing the communication. Add to this the complexities of modern conversation by text messages and emails and you have a recipe for disaster!

Communication is made up of many things, including action, body language, speech and intent. If you are just hearing what is being said, you are missing out on many parts of the communication and this is where problems arise. Try to listen to communications you receive with your intuition.

For example, if someone you love is often nagging you, use your intuition and 'listen' for what the real communication is. A friend of mine used to visit his mother every few weeks. Every time he walked in the door his mother would start up with questions like: have you got a girlfriend yet? What are you doing with your life? You look too skinny—are you eating properly?

This incessant nagging caused frustration and arguments from as far back as he could remember, until the day he realised that her communication was not the words she was saying. Her communication was that she loved him and wanted him to be happy. From that moment, every time he 'heard' the nagging questions he would listen to his gut, smile and respond, 'I love you too Mum', and she would smile and say, 'Good'.

If you have relationships where the conversations do not work, try listening for the whole of the communication rather than just the words. You may be surprised how different the message is! By bringing this skill to your new business venture you will bring a heightened level of understanding to your relationships with partners, clients and service providers.

Challenge yourself

Personal development is very important when it comes to honing your intuition skills. There are thousands of ways you can expand yourself and grow as a person, including: travel, meditation, courses, retreats, books and DVDs, all manner of adventures, public speaking and starting a business.

Anything that puts you out of your comfort zone will help you grow as a person. Experiences such as starting a new job, moving to a new country or bringing home your first baby create a heightened sense of awareness. Have you noticed that when you are out of your comfort zone things sometimes look different? Putting yourself in challenging situations and environments will give you more opportunities to listen for what your gut is telling you and act upon it. It is exactly in the moments of not knowing how things work that we want to be able to trust our gut — grabbing opportunities that challenge you will give you plenty of practice.

Starting your dream business is the perfect way to learn! It is worth sticking with the exciting goals that make you feel a little uncomfortable because you gain confidence, inspiration, self-expression and self-awareness. All these things will contribute to the peace you need to listen to and trust your intuition, as well as a greater capacity for satisfaction and happiness.

The wrap-up

There will always be bumps in the road, especially if you are putting yourself out there to achieve the things that are important to you. You can't control what challenges come up, but you can control how you deal with them. Your mindset will be the difference between success and failure, and will dictate your experience of life and the opportunities that present themselves to you. Take on these mindset tips for success and your dream lifestyle will be closer than you think. Remember to:

- Recognise the condition of analysis paralysis so that you can spot if you have the symptoms.

- Put your fear into perspective — distinguish any real danger from chemical trickery, and act accordingly.

- Always act like anything is possible; take all the actions you know to take and be open for incredible things to happen that are outside of your control.

- Persist, persist and persist until you get the results you are looking for.

⮞ Practise creating your own luck.

⮞ Develop selective hearing—get your encouragement from those who support your goals.

⮞ Accept that failure will happen from time to time and use it as an opportunity to reflect and grow.

⮞ Be abundantly generous.

⮞ Quiet the noise in your head and develop the habit of listening to and trusting your intuition.

Chapter 4

Finding your passion

Defining and working on something you are passionate about is so important it deserves its own chapter. So here it is! As well as being another tip for success, it is the foundation for my whole philosophy about lifestyle income.

In this chapter we will look at:

➪ the importance of choosing something you're passionate about

➪ unearthing your passions

➪ a step-by-step process for creating valuable business ideas from your passions and interests.

Why you should choose a passion-based business

Why is passion so important? The reason I focus on passion is that when you do something you are absolutely passionate about you are far more likely to succeed. Creating your dream lifestyle is a challenge, and the more you love what you do the more likely you are to stick with it when things get tough.

Think about it this way: how many 'get-rich-quick' schemes or shortcuts to wealth have you heard of? Unless you have been hiding under a rock, you are probably exposed to them on a regular basis. Aside from the fact that many such schemes are questionable, anyone who has started and succeeded in business will tell you that you need massive amounts of determination —and that can be hard to maintain when you're selling someone else's fad or miracle product for the hope of future wealth.

Other than a lucky break like winning the lottery, I haven't found any shortcuts to great wealth. You will, however, always find a whole lot of sharks ready to take your money when you go looking!

While there are lots of genuine opportunities all around you, you need determination to carry you through when things get hard—as they often do in business. This is why it is important to choose a business that you really love, that suits your values and that has the potential to give you the lifestyle you are looking for.

Here lies the problem: people are often unclear about what they really want from life. We often ignore our passions because we don't have time to pursue them or we don't think it's possible to achieve them, and so we don't make goals that take them into account.

Your passion personality

When it comes to passion and lifestyle, there are three types of personality.

Passion Seekers

Passion Seekers are the people who are out there either trying to make it happen or who are actually making it happen. They seem to live with purpose and be taking action on the things that are important to them. They will have their fair share of successes as well as failures, which you will hear about because they are giving it a go. The people you admire and wish to emulate are probably Passion Seekers who have had success with their ventures and adventures.

The General Masses

The General Masses are going through life with what they are passionate about being somewhere out there in the undefined future—they will get to it tomorrow, or maybe the next day. Many such people will miss out on opportunities to create a lifestyle they desire. They may or may not be setting themselves up for financial security and wealth.

These people are good at ignoring or discounting their passions using a number of excuses, such as they don't have enough time, it's too much of a luxury or it's just not possible. Sometimes they push their dreams so far down the priority list that they actually forget they wanted to do them in the first place. However, they do get temporarily motivated when something reminds them of their passions every once in a while—a wistful moment of what could be.

People in this category sometimes take a leap and become a Passion Seeker (often after a life change or good life crisis). Or they may take a risk, get burnt and become a Safe Operator.

Safe Operators

Safe Operators are the people who actively avoid even acknowledging what they really want from life in case it doesn't happen. They avoid any sort of situation that puts them at risk of failing. They play it safe with small, achievable goals, and life ticks along. Safe Operators often become very good at what they do and crave familiar situations and people.

Unfortunately for them the best things in life generally require putting yourself in a situation where you can't control everything. For example, you have to be vulnerable and risk being hurt before you can have a wonderfully loving relationship.

The risks you must take are proportional to the opportunities and successes you want to create. If you are not willing to take risks, your chances of reaching (or even having) exciting goals are much reduced.

Which one are you?

Can you recognise yourself as one of those personalities? Or are you a combination of two?

What is often surprising for many Passion Seekers is how simple it is to include their passions into their lifestyle. It is amazing how far focus and determination will take you when you actually identify what you want to do and what is important to you. Your passion and perseverance are the fuel for success, and those who dare stand up and challenge themselves to get the most out of life are the ones who get propelled the furthest.

I have been fortunate to meet a lot of people who have decided to pursue their passions and their big goals in life. It is amazing to watch people's attitudes, emotions and experience of the world change because of this. I see people who have a type of energy and purpose about them, which they hadn't experienced before. This is something that is thrilling to witness. These people have crossed the imaginary line between those who realise it is possible to accomplish great things and are willing to give it a go and those who are more concerned with the possibility that they may not succeed. Rather than being focused on everyday issues, people who are having a go at fulfilling their passions are talking about an opportunity that just came up, the next big goal, how they overcame the last challenge and how great life is.

The best bit about pursuing your passions, however, is your experience of life. When you are pursuing goals that are important to you, you start to buzz and really feel alive! Bring purpose to your actions and life starts to seem electric, your energy levels rise, your ability to take things on and deal with challenges increases and you find the doors opening to exciting opportunities that were not possible before you put yourself out there.

Sometimes you see people who appear to be doing the work of many and they manage it with grace and ease. These are generally the people who feel that they are living with purpose. They are pursuing their passions, and they are a force to be reckoned with.

What makes your heart sing?

What are you passionate about? What makes your heart sing? When do you feel most alive, fulfilled and happy? This is something personal to each of us.

Quite often our passions and lifestyle goals change over time. What was your dream when you were five? To be a fireman, a pilot or a singer? How about when you were 15, and 25? Some of us will have a common theme for our passions which lasts our whole lives, and some of us have passions that change every few years, or every few months!

Take some time to think about what you are passionate about now. What do you spend a lot of time doing, reading about, researching or discussing? What makes you smile and daydream?

If you are having a little trouble figuring out what you are passionate about, try answering the following questions.

- What subjects do you talk about a lot?
- What are your hobbies, or what would you like to spend more time doing?
- How would you spend your time if you didn't need money?
- If you could be anywhere, where would you be and what would you be doing?
- What do you dream about doing with your life?
- What industry would you love to be involved in?

If you're still stuck, close your eyes and imagine what your perfect life would look like. Where would you be? Who would you be with? What would you be achieving? Now write your list of passions in your notebook. These are the areas we are going to look at in more detail as we work towards creating an internet business for you.

Creating goals and defining time frames

When I ask people what they are passionate about, I often find that what they come up with has nothing to do with what they do for a living or what they spend their time doing. The next part of this chapter will take you through the steps you need to take to find value in your passions so you can turn them into something real and generate an income from them.

The first step is to set some goals and some time frames for achieving them. Your goal is the end point—the destination. Goals give you a clear target at which to aim all of your efforts and actions. Without goals, it is likely that you will lack focus in your approach.

Time frames are equally as important. Without them your goals can slip into the 'someday' category. The energy you put towards a goal will be driven by your deadline—have you ever crammed for an exam or finished a project at the last minute? You are not alone! A clear time frame will dictate your focus and energy. Consider what might be involved, including how much spare time you have and your other commitments. But don't think too much! Analysis paralysis is ready and waiting. If you find that your time frames are too short, you always have the option of changing them. It is far better to need to extend a time frame than to give yourself far too much time and not start for months. If you are like many people, you will leave it to the last minute regardless of how long you give yourself. So create urgency and momentum with a tight but achievable deadline.

If you are embarking on a brand-new goal in a brand-new field with no idea how you are going to make it work, there is never a right time frame because anything could happen! So, choose a time frame that will motivate you and get you started. For example, I had no idea how I was going to fulfil my business goal in 12 months. Imagine if it took 14 months or 13 months instead of 12; do you think I would have been upset? No! The important thing was that my deadline got me started. Making it 12 months (as opposed to a number of years) forced me to take it very seriously, be very creative and not waste any time. If I had too long a time frame (such as five years) or no time frame at all I would not be where I am today. I would still be planning my first move.

Have a go. Think of the goals you want to set for yourself and define the time frame in which you plan to achieve each goal. Make a list of your goals and include a deadline. I have shown a few of my own below as an example.

Goal	By when
1 Pack up and leave Australia for indefinite travel	August 2011
2 Become a dive master	December 2012
3 Write three books that inspire people to make the most of life	September 2013

In creating these goals for my life and declaring a time frame for their achievement I immediately started to think about how I would go about achieving them. The time frames made each goal more real and gave me an incentive. Within each goal and time frame a series of actions emerged that I would need to take, and with that a series of deadlines for the achievement of each of those actions became clear.

So take your list, make it look important and place it where you will see it every day. You can add to your list over time or make changes to it if your priorities change.

Next we're going to focus on how you can use your passions to create an income, and how blogging makes this all possible.

Sharing your passion on the internet

The internet gives us a platform for sharing our work, experiences, art, challenges and just about anything else. With the creation of the internet, information sharing has become an abundant and common feature of our lives. The net provides easy access for us to upload material for other people to find.

One of the most common ways to share information is through a blog. The word 'blog' is a combination of the words web and log, and indicates regularly posted content, whether it is formal or informal, personal or corporate. Blogs are more interactive than pages on other types of websites because people can usually interact with the writer by making comments, and readers over time build a relationship with the blogger.

What *is* a blog?

People can become confused because the word *blog* is used in three ways. A blog can be:

- a type of stand-alone website with its own domain name and host

- a part of a website; for example, a company may have a corporate website with a subdomain that is the blog

- an individual post on a blog; you blog on your blog (get it?).

In the first option the blog is a website in its own right, and that is what we will be focusing on as the core of a passion-based internet business.

Why blogging?

Blogging is becoming an increasingly popular and convenient way to share information, opinions, experiences, personal challenges and so on. Blogs have a personality of their own determined by the content that is posted, and they will attract an audience with an appreciation for the content.

Blogs are great for people wanting to create a long-term internet presence on a subject they are passionate about because:

➵ *They require regular new content.* A blog by its nature is a regular source of new content for readers. Whether you post daily, weekly or fortnightly, the blogs on your blog (yes, it can be confusing!) are designed to build on themselves and will add more and more value to your website over time as you build and grow.

➵ *You can build a database over time.* A blog gives people a reason to subscribe to your site and to come back to read your content on a regular basis. A growing database is one of the most valuable assets for anyone looking to make money online.

➵ *You can build relationships.* Bloggers can develop close relationships with their readers and build a huge following over time. People will start to feel that they know you through what you share.

A blog is not the only type of website you can use to create income on the internet, but it is the foundation for the philosophy in this book. Whether your blog is formal, fancy, casual or funny, you can use it to share your passions, build a database and ultimately create income.

Turning your knowledge into value

This is the fun bit! Look back at your notes from the exercise where you identified what you are passionate about. It's now time to see how you can use those passions on the internet to provide value for other people. I have said before that your knowledge, experiences and skills are valuable, but what does that mean? Does this mean *any* knowledge, skill or experience can be used to make money online?

The answer is … wait for it … yes! *Anything* that you have learned will give you topics that you can share to inform, inspire or entertain. Whether your experience is in fixing a car, theatre costumes, playing poker, dealing with difficult people, surviving an illness, cooking Asian food, renting out a house or making natural baby food, you have an opportunity to share your knowledge with others through your own website. For example, think about the following:

🐀 Do you have experience in an industry that has a fashionable or cool image, such as music or travel?

🐀 Have you suffered from an illness and found ways to alleviate the symptoms?

🐀 Have you had success in fundraising or making money?

🐀 Do you have a child with special needs?

🐀 Have you learned a lot about natural health or sustainable living?

🐀 Do you have a passion for fitness, motorcycles, doll house furniture, coffee or finding bargains *ad infinitum*

🐀 Do you know how to coach a sport?

🐀 Do you know hundreds of special family recipes?

🐀 Are you embarking on a huge personal challenge?

This list is just the beginning. And, really, all these questions can be simplified down to this: do you know *anything at all about anything* that other people would be interested in? If you can't answer yes to this, think harder!

I have come across hundreds of brave and creative people who are taking their passions and experiences and creating new sources of income by sharing them on the internet. For example: Nikki Johnston makes and sells custom-designed keepsakes and jewellery through her website Oh My Giddy Aunt. She sells them along with gorgeous stories for each piece, and all things fairies, celebrations and special occasions.

Marta Davidovich Ockuly shares her love of positivity and quotes on her website Joy of Quotes. She creates income through the sale of her products and by recommending third-party products.

Take a moment to think about the millions and millions —and *millions*—of searches people do through Google and other search engines every day. People from all over the world ask weird and wonderful questions every minute, and for every question it is hoped that someone, somewhere has posted a good answer on a website. And what about you? What are some of the things you searched for recently? If you are like me, no topic is too large or small for a Google search, and I almost always find what I am looking for. This is the magic of the internet; every time you share your experiences and knowledge you add to its value and usefulness for those looking for information, inspiration, opinions and advice.

Now it's time for you to take your passions, knowledge and experience and turn them into ideas of value on the internet. Take a clean page and draw a website ideas table, like this:

	Idea 1	Idea 2	etc.
Passion, knowledge and experience			
Community wants/needs			
Practical skills			
Website ideas for value			
Opportunities/ resources			

In this exercise you will start to clarify all of the possible ways in which your experiences, passions and knowledge can be valuable to others on the internet. As this is an initial brainstorm, let your creative juices flow! There are no wrong answers, and the more ideas you can list the better.

First, list your passions one by one in the first row. In the same row, add any knowledge, experience and expertise you have. Include personal challenges you have overcome, your achievements and things that you find easy but other people may find difficult to learn or do. You may look to your career or hobbies, or things that you do well naturally.

Once you have filled out the first row with as many points as you can, think about the next row on community wants and needs, taking into account your list in the first row. Community wants and needs are areas where you think your passion, experience or knowledge could benefit a particular community (a community being a group of potential consumers). You could benefit them by providing information, inspiration, advice, entertainment or a service. Think about possible gaps in the market, or problems that a particular community may experience.

Next, in the practical skills row add all the practical skills you could bring to a website business in each area you listed in the first row. It could be anything, from personal skills such as communication, networking and sales to technical skills like photography, writing, website development or video editing. The list is basically infinite; add any skills you think may help your business.

For the website ideas for value row, think how you could provide value by sharing your knowledge or experience with each community via a blog. Think about what you could include on the site, and how you would share it with the audience (for example, through writing, videos or audio). Think about who the audience is. Think about the experience they would have coming to the website and why they would want to come back often.

Last but not least, for the final row brainstorm any opportunities and resources that could give you a preference for a particular idea for creating value; for example, upcoming events, contacts in that industry or groups in that community who could spread the word for you.

Complete each row for each idea you have, and by the end you should have several ideas with good potential for a theme for a new income-generating blog. Even if you already have something in mind, explore all the options so that you have a good selection to choose from.

As an example, here is the table for what became Grassroots Internet Strategy:

Passion, knowledge and experience	How to set up and structure a business website for success. My experience is coaching small business owners in everything from the minor details to the big picture.
Community wants/needs	Small business owners need a fast return on their website investment, so it is important that they understand how to achieve that. They want to use their website to grow their business and be more profitable.
Practical skills	Coaching and motivating people; writing; networking; social media.
Website ideas for value	Create a website for small business owners, with lots of information specifically for them on how to set up and maintain a website that will help them reach their goals. We could offer courses and resources that help to condense all of the information on the website and answer all the questions they may have.
Opportunities/ resources	My existing clients and community. My involvement in some strong internet-based communities of small business owners. A potential business partner with complementary skills and interests.

Once you have completed your own table, take a look through your points and start to explore each idea further. You will find that some stand out as really interesting or exciting and some will seem less interesting or just plain boring! Work with each idea until you are ready to either drop it or take the next step with it. If you have a few that you love, consider what opportunities you have for each one. If one has a huge community that you can leverage in the short term, it may be a good place to start. Ultimately, you should trust your gut and go with the idea that most excites you.

At this point it may not seem obvious how you can create income from these ideas, but don't worry—we will cover that soon. At this point there is no wrong idea, unless it doesn't sing to you. Does the thought of having a web business based on this topic excite you? If the answer is yes, it is a good place to start.

Where are you now?

Generally my clients at this point are in one of three spaces.

⇨ They know what they want to do, what their passion, knowledge and experiences are and what they want to share.

⇨ They have many exciting ideas but are not quite ready to choose just one.

⇨ They haven't quite got their heads around it because they need to know how it works first.

If you are in the third category, don't despair! Finish reading the book to see how it all fits together and then come back to the exercises in this chapter and try again!

The wrap-up

When creating a business, your passion for the area you have chosen can make or break it. There will always be seemingly great opportunities to make money, but if you are going to start something new you would be smart to start something that you are thrilled to be involved in. Remember to:

⮫ Avoid the sharks! There is a whole industry profiting from those who are out to get something for nothing.

⮫ Let yourself be a Passion Seeker, to be bold in creating a business and lifestyle that you find thrilling. It is possible if you are really willing to do what it takes.

⮫ Find what makes your heart sing and then set goals and timelines that will have you taking action now.

⮫ Make the most of the massive opportunities the internet gives you to share your passions. Through blogging, anyone with a commitment to providing value can create a community of like-minded people.

⮫ Be creative about what it is you can share that would be of value. Using the website ideas table, explore all of your passions, skills and knowledge and develop lots of ideas to choose from.

Chapter 5

How to make money online

We've finally arrived at the bit you've been waiting for: how to generate your own low-maintenance income so that you can retire!

You will be pleased to know that there are several ways you can make money online. In this chapter I outline the most common, popular and effective ways to generate income using the internet, some of which can be the basis for how you can create income.

For bloggers I suggest you start with two main methods: recommending affiliate products and the sale of digital products. However, it is also important that you understand what else is out there. Over time you can take a multifaceted approach to generating revenue, as some things will work better for your business than others. It all depends on the community you build around your website and how well you execute your plan.

Income generation in the digital world

The world of online sales and income generation is as much about the number and type of people who visit your website, the number of subscribers you generate and the actions they take while visiting your site as it is about sales. The internet is a world of abundance, which is not surprising with an estimated 1.8 billion users.

If you provide consistently high quality content, are willing to continuously learn about internet marketing and have a decent helping of good old-fashioned determination, you too can grow an alternative source of income online from something that you love.

It is important to understand how money goes around online so that you can start to understand how each website you visit supports itself. What will make the big difference is your ability to create a database of interested subscribers, which you grow steadily over time. The more people you have on your database the more chances you have to create an income. I will repeat this point throughout the rest of the book as it is essential to your success.

How to make money online

Here is the lowdown on bringing in the bucks.

Selling advertising space

The first thing people often think about when they consider how to make money through the internet is selling advertising space. Contrary to popular belief, *building a good website does not necessarily mean that you can make a lot of money from advertising*.

If you have a niche website that is recognised in the industry, and which has a high volume of traffic, then there is money to be made selling advertising. However, the reality is that very few websites make enough from advertising alone to be sustainable, and most small business websites do not get a look in.

Internet advertising is a whole industry of its own. It is complex and run by media agencies that are experts at linking highly successful websites with corporate clients and their big budgets. Your value to media agencies will depend on your ability to attract large numbers of visitors in a certain geographical area, successfully specialise in a certain niche and present an attractive and professional website and products.

If you want to set up your own advertising model separate to the media agencies, you could sell space to individual smaller companies. This can be profitable but it requires an on-going, personal sales process. If you are working on your own, this will take time away from developing and marketing your website.

Unless you have a unique model for advertising that eliminates much of the personal work required, or a dedicated salesperson who can sell to and manage your clients, consider that advertising as a revenue option will probably not be viable until you have solid, significant and targeted traffic.

For example, Robert Gerrish set up Flying Solo to provide information and resources to the micro-business community in Australia. In addition, he set up a forum where the community of people interested in micro-business could directly exchange ideas, information and assistance. Gerrish intended to have an advertising model from the outset, and worked hard to develop a quality niche website that attracted large numbers of visitors and members. As Flying Solo established their value and popularity in the niche they became interesting to media agencies, and now advertising is a core part of their revenue generation.

Sponsorship

Sponsorship is the trade of products, services or money in exchange for association with your website. Sponsors are looking to associate their name with yours with the people that know you, primarily your visitors and subscribers. Sponsorship deals start at the low end, such as free hosting of your website in exchange for a badge on your site, or donating prizes to your competitions in exchange for logo placement or a mention. At the top end, think large cash sponsorship for the live feed of a major sporting event. And then there's everything in between.

If you want to make the most of sponsorship, do your research and understand who will be looking at your website and which companies pursue the same target audience. When you have found a company or group of companies that you think may benefit from exposure to your consumers, approach them with an offer.

For example, Belle and Nick from Moving 2 London created a handy eBook guide for people planning to move to London which recommended companies such as travel agencies, job agencies and hostels. They approached each of these types of companies and suggested a small fee from each of them to be included as a sponsor of the eBook. They attracted five sponsors, which covered the costs of production before they launched. They also arranged for each sponsor to help with promotion of the eBook, and every business was able to benefit from the cross promotion.

Find companies whose products are aimed at your target visitors and you have the opportunity to create valuable partnerships. For example, Charlotte Squire from Happyzine collects prizes from sponsors who want to promote their eco products to her database of subscribers. She offers these as incentives for new subscribers to join her website database, and the eco products get mentioned and sometimes reviewed as part of the competition. The subscribers get a chance to win a great prize, the sponsor company has its products viewed by thousands of potential customers and Happyzine gets to increase the size of their database — everyone is happy!

Look for how you can leverage your website for the benefit of other companies, websites or organisations and then contact the ones that would make a good fit. Be clear about the benefits you offer potential sponsors when you approach them.

Affiliate ads and Google AdSense

Now we will look at the art of hosting adverts for other companies. The adverts can be text based, images or banners which appear somewhere on a page on your website.

Google's program AdSense analyses the content on your website and posts corresponding ads, or places ads based on your users' interests and previous internet behaviour. Other programs, such as clixGalore and Commission Junction, allow you to pick the ads yourself through their ad marketplace.

There are a few models for such advertising:

☞ CPC (cost per click) — you make a certain amount of money each time someone clicks on the ad on your site; for example, Google AdSense.

☞ CPA (cost per action) — you make money when someone clicks through from your website and performs a particular action on the advertiser's site, such as subscribing to a newsletter or requesting further information.

☞ Commission — you make money from the sales generated from the traffic you send to the merchant.

If you are considering hosting ads, there are a few things to think about:

☞ Make sure the product and service adverts you host fit with the type of image and values you are aiming to portray on your website and are what you would be happy to advertise personally.

For example, it may not be a good fit for a website about teen pregnancy to host adverts for mortgage refinance or a healthy living website to advertise a fast food chain. If your website provides practical tips for improving the environment, an ad for a major soft drink company will seem out of place.

✎ Consider how the ads will affect the look and feel of your website. Ads can make a website look cheap and unappealing if not done well.

✎ Ads create a major conflict. You want people to focus on the content you are sharing on your site, whereas the intention of an ad is to attract attention away from your content.

✎ Consider that with an ad you are directing your visitors to go elsewhere. In the early days it can take a lot of work to get people to find and visit your website; do you really want them to leave again by clicking on an ad? Even if you get paid for them to click, weigh that up against the actual cost in your effort, time and money to get them to visit you in the first place — it may be higher than you think.

If you do have a lot of traffic, a growing membership or people who visit your site religiously and you are happy for them to leave your site (because you know they will come back), this form of advertising may be more appealing as an addition to your other revenue-generating activities. However, if you have a single, content-rich website, this type of marketing by itself is not likely to make you rich, or even pay the bills, until you have built up a large flow of traffic.

Affiliate marketing

Affiliate marketing is an arrangement to promote someone else's product or service on your website or to your database. When people click through from your website or email and purchase a product, you are paid a commission on that sale. Affiliate programs offer commissions ranging from 3 per cent to 75 per cent of the purchase price, depending on the arrangement and type of product. It can be a healthy source of income for online marketers if you have a large database or lots of traffic and you do a great job with your recommendations. I have even found that some of my competitors have become affiliates and promote me and my products.

One of the largest online affiliate marketplaces is ClickBank. It enables you to compare thousands of products in a huge variety of areas. There are other smaller marketplaces as well, and plenty of businesses that have an independent affiliate program.

Once you have registered with an affiliate program you will be issued with a unique hoplink, which is the link you use in your promotions of that product. When your visitors click the link they are diverted through to the sales page of the product where they can make a purchase. Once they make a purchase, your account will be credited in accordance with that program. Most programs pay every 30 days if you have earned a minimum payout amount (for example, $100), otherwise commissions will roll over to following months until they accumulate to the payout threshold. A word of warning: if you have the link wrong, or do not have your affiliate ID in the hoplink, the sale will not be attributed to you and you will miss out on the commission, so check your links carefully!

Sometimes there are stand-down periods where membership programs are involved (for example, commissions are paid only after the new customer has been a member for three months) or there are other conditions for payment, so make sure you read the terms of the program. The larger marketplaces will look after all the financial transactions, so you are not relying on an independent business owner to report to and pay you, which can be a benefit.

When looking for good products to recommend, keep your eyes peeled for any products in your industry that people rave about or any that you personally find amazing. These are the ones that you want to recommend, so check out their websites and see if they have an affiliate program.

Be sure to only recommend quality products you have tested or know to be good, because people visiting your website trust *you* when they act on your recommendations. Some companies will give you a sample of the product so that you can review it before you recommend it, otherwise buy it and check it out.

If you have a loyal database of people who have been visiting your website, email them a great and honest review of the product that you have written personally.

You will find that some affiliate products are more popular than others. Keep those that do well and ditch those that do not, replacing them with other recommended products.

Until you have a healthy amount of traffic and subscribers, this type of revenue generation can seem slow at first but will gain momentum in line with your database or number of visitors. This form of revenue generation can be very lucrative so it is worth testing it from the outset with your new website. Your success will depend on your choosing affiliate products and services that suit your website's visitors and the people on your database, as well as your skill with writing compelling reviews or recommendations. Place affiliate marketing high on your list of revenue-generating activities.

Donations

If you are providing something of informational, technical or entertainment value to others, such as music, widgets or applications, you could try offering users the option to 'make a donation', 'buy me a beer' or 'buy me a coffee'. Widgets are mini applications that perform a certain basic function, such as a clock, a calculator or a subscription form. Developers create the code and make it available to website owners to install on their websites. Requesting donations is popular with web developers who have developed freeware, and they will offer a chance to make a donation right before you download the application.

Of course, traditionally donations are collected by charities and not-for-profits. For example, Avaaz ask for donations towards their general administration as well as campaigns they are running for environmental or social justice causes.

PayPal offers very simple ways to collect donations. They give you code to paste on your website that gives your visitors buttons for making donations. You can ask for a single donation or a monthly commitment.

Your success with collecting donations will depend on the level of emotional buy-in your visitors have with you, as well as why you are asking for money. If you have a worthwhile project that people want to be involved in or if you have created a huge amount of value in your sharing of content and ask for support for a certain goal, you will find that you have more luck than simply adding a donation button and asking people to support the website.

Paid membership and paid add-value services

Paid membership works by charging a regular or one-off fee in exchange for providing access to content or services. Your ability to develop a successful membership-based website relates directly to the value of the information or services that you have to offer. If you plan to offer membership, make sure the content and benefits that members can access are significantly more valuable than anything you offer at no cost.

Dating websites are a classic example. They usually offer free content to draw you in, such as your ability to create a profile and contact a certain number of people, and then paid content once you see that you might get in touch with some potential dates. The dating model downfall, however, is that once customers get what they want (a relationship) they no longer need their membership! This is why internet dating services are always advertising.

Having a membership service requires a big commitment. You need to maintain the value of the additional content and develop robust systems and infrastructure for managing your membership, as well as marketing it well so that the website is visited. If you really want to introduce membership but are on a tight budget, consider adding a membership or add-value model down the track once you have proven content and consumers who value you.

Robert from Flying Solo created a free membership from the outset, introducing an add-value opportunity several years later that gives his existing members more chances to promote their business. This way they are able to keep their free members happy and give those who want extra benefits the chance to enjoy a VIP service.

Selling products or services

One of the common reasons people set up a business website is to sell their products and services. Unlike a physical shop or office, the set-up costs for starting an internet business are extremely low, with the opportunity to sell to a global audience.

Websites that sell products or services need to:

➯ have an e-commerce facility that allows tracking of sales and processing of orders; for example, have a look at E-Junkie

➯ be set up for receiving payments with a payment service such as PayPal

➯ make customers feel safe and secure enough to provide their personal information and credit card details.

In the beginning, if you only have a few products or services your e-commerce facility may be as simple as a self-coded button from E-Junkie linked to a payment service such as PayPal. These applications allow you to enter your product details, prices and so on, and they will produce code that you can paste into your website.

Whatever your method for customer purchases it is important that the process looks, and is, legitimate. Although making purchases on the internet has become common practice, you do not want to give people a reason to doubt your credibility. Make sure you use professionally presented and well-known payment applications.

Test your purchase system from time to time to make sure that it is straightforward and that it looks professional. This includes using your website name or full name for the account, and not that bizarre nickname you have been using since high school!

Have a clear and compelling call to action on every page. A call to action is the request you are making of people reading that page, such as 'Subscribe to my newsletter', 'Download my eBook' or 'Buy now'. It is the action that you want them to take. If you decide to include an incentive for potential customers, make it something of value.

If you have a niche service, make it easy for people to see what they will get when they do business with you. Katherine West, for example, shows her passion for painting animals, pets and landscapes. On her website Kty West she commissions her work and advertises her prints. She has a unique personal service, and it is important that she has images of previous commissions available for potential customers to view.

Generating sales leads

Another common reason that business owners produce a website is to generate sales leads. A sales lead is when a customer calls the business or enters his or her details into a form so that the business owner can contact them. This will appeal to people whose businesses are service-based, like a plumber or equipment hire company. A website to generate sales leads would also appeal for products and services that require a more personal effort in selling—for example, cars, carpets or coaching—and other items or services that a customer would want to view or trial before purchasing.

When looking to generate sales leads it is important that you give visitors plenty of reasons to contact you. As always, have clear calls to action on every page of your website. Create quality information (website copy) about your products and services that includes all their benefits and a reason to act now.

Although I focus on digital products and affiliate products in this book, you can also use your website to advertise any services that you offer as well. You may find your ability to provide a service will increase your cash flow and enable you to leave your job more quickly. If you know good service providers that would benefit your visitors, you may also choose to outsource services as part of your income-generation plan.

 Case study: Grassroots Internet Strategy

At Grassroots we work with four different types of revenue generation.

The sale of digital products

From the beginning we were committed to creating quality products that would benefit small business owners. As a result, we have spent a lot of time creating products that we feel are extremely valuable to our customers. We slowly add to our offering when we have time to create new products, and we update existing ones from time to time if parts of them become outdated. Our product sales increase as our subscribers grow, and as word of mouth spreads in the small business community.

We created an affiliate program so that other people could recommend our products and receive a 50 per cent commission on any sales they refer for us.

Services

Both Melinda and I were already service providers, so we used the website to market our existing services and continued to provide services until our incomes increased through the website. Our service packages directly relate to the content on the website, and include general internet strategy for small business as well as several specialty internet marketing services such as search engine optimisation, copy writing, social media marketing, custom blog creation and e-mail newsletter production.

Outsourced services

In the process of building our Grassroots website we established a relationship with WordPress developer Tessa Needham. We found that the mix of her development knowledge with our marketing knowledge made for a very rounded package for new website owners. So we packaged this and made it available for our consumers and outsourced Tessa's part. This was not our intention from the beginning but it worked very well and became very handy for our growth in the first few months.

Affiliates

Later we started to add some recommended affiliate products and services from companies that we had dealt with and loved. We are very transparent when promoting affiliate products and have a policy of only recommending things we use ourselves.

From time to time we mention affiliate products in review posts and list the most useful ones with other resources we recommend on our 'Tools' page.

Finding what works for your business

As you can see there are plenty of different ways to create income on the internet. I suggest you take a rounded approach, testing a few options to see what works best for your website visitors and subscribers. Some of these options will be perfect for you and your business and some will not. Some will work in the short term but most will work better in the long term. When you are learning the ropes, some things may fail at first before you succeed, so hang in there.

There are a few things that make revenue-generating activities successful: the amount of traffic or number of subscribers you have, the presentation of your offers, the appropriateness of your offers to your audience, the perceived value of your offers and the manner in which you sell and distribute. For this reason it is worth testing and testing (and testing!) your revenue options as you grow until you are happy with the results.

Providing value

The key to website success is value. Whether you provide entertainment, opportunity, information or inspiration, whether your website is targeted at teenagers or horticulturists, fashion queens or rocket scientists, people will revisit your site, recommend your site or subscribe to your site based on the value they get from it.

The more you share, the more well known you will become and the more opportunities you will have to create income. Give everything you have; don't hold back. You want to develop trust and a rapport with your readers. You want to create value every time they visit your website. If the information is what people want they will keep coming back. If what you share is valuable, people will subscribe. If you provide value to them on a regular basis then you have the opportunity to make offers to a captured audience of people who trust you.

How do you judge website value?

As you already know, value is subjective. In this next exercise we look at what you consider valuable about some of your favourite websites so that you can practise gauging your own work. If you already have a website, do the same exercise with your own website as if you were a new visitor.

Type in the URL of the website you want to analyse. Think about the following issues:

➥ Will the content on the site benefit me? How?

➥ Do I feel compelled to read the content, look at the images, watch videos or take a next step? Why?

➥ Are there links to other places on the site that I may find intriguing?

➥ Does it answer questions that I may have?

➥ Do I want to buy the products being sold? Why?

➥ How do they encourage me to take an action or come back?

Now take a look at the website as a returning customer or regular user and ask yourself these questions:

➭ Why would I return to the site regularly? (Is there regular new content, news, updates, forums, a blog?)

➭ What do I receive if I subscribe to the database or sign up for membership?

➭ How often could I come to the site and get value from it?

➭ Can I participate in the website? Do I feel that I can contribute to it?

Many business owners make the mistake of creating a website with a great design that simply provides information about the business. This may be interesting for someone who wants exactly what you are selling, but only until they make the decision to buy or not, at which point your information has been consumed … next!

Create a plan to add new value to your site on a regular basis so that people have good reason to visit you time and time again.

What value can I provide?

Let's have a look at how you can provide value.

➭ *Information.* Share your knowledge and experience (as well as other people's) in the form of news, articles, blogs, interviews, video clips and reviews. Write about topics that will interest the people who fit the target audience you want. If you don't want to write or produce the content yourself, you can source content from other people and organisations in the industry.

➭ *Entertainment.* Provide your audience with videos, quizzes, polls, audio, interviews, images and opinions that will entertain them. Look at what would appeal to your target audience and create content or collate other people's content. An obvious source of videos, for example, is

YouTube, where you will find a goldmine of content on a huge range of subjects.

✏ *Opportunities*. You can offer webcasts or eBooks, specialist services, access to special industry updates, networking or interacting with like-minded individuals, giving your visitors opportunities that they may not get elsewhere.

✏ *Inspiration*. You can inspire people in any way: stories, videos, quotes, positive news or documenting a personal challenge — the list goes on.

Think about your frequency of posts, the type of posts and the topics. Your consistency with frequency and quality content is what will attract and keep subscribers who enjoy your style. So decide whether you will be updating your content daily, weekly or fortnightly, and stick with it.

It is okay to mix up the types of media that you use as different people have different preferences and find value in different things. Just remember the magic rules: be consistent and provide value!

What is your competition like?

Who else is doing it?

One big, fat fallacy in business is that you can only be successful with something that hasn't been done before. While this can be a huge benefit, it is certainly not essential and can sometimes be detrimental. While you do need to have a unique selling point, your website does not have to be the first of its kind. Imagine if we only had one lifestyle website, for example — how boring the world would be! While the information you offer will in some ways be similar to other information that is available, what sets it apart is that *you* created it — and there is nobody else in the world like you, with your perspective, view, knowledge, experience or design aesthetic! When I was learning about internet marketing I must have read 20 books, subscribed to several blogs and attended a few courses. Most of the things I read conveyed similar messages but each was presented in a different way in the voice of a person with different experiences. This is one of the benefits of being in the information business; more often than not your unique selling point is *you*—your experience, opinion and the delivery of information which only you can create.

Have a look at who else is marketing similar information on the internet. Seek out your competition. Subscribe to their blogs and buy their products. Look at what they are doing well and what you think they could improve on.

Following are a couple of questions you should ask when deciding who your competition is and then assessing how useful they can be to you.

Does it appear to be a well-developed industry?

The way that you interact with your industry will in part depend on how many others there are like you. The benefit of starting in an industry that is popular, with plenty of websites delivering information, is that other people before you have already set the bar and educated the public on what to expect and hopefully what to pay for. For example, our industry (internet marketing) is absolutely packed; however, people are used to paying for quality digital products. The way to operate successfully in a packed industry is to make strategic alliances, try new approaches with delivery and chip away at your niche with consistent, quality content.

The benefit of starting in an industry that has very few players is that you have the opportunity to establish your website as the place to go. It is a lot easier to be a big fish when there aren't many other fish to compare you to.

How successful are they?

How successful do you think they are? Be a detective and analyse their websites; are there signs of loyal visitors? Do you think they are making many sales? Does it seem like they provide a valuable resource?

One of the fabulous things about the internet is that even your direct competition can be an ally and you can benefit from each other's products through affiliate marketing. You can refer your people to their products and make a commission, and vice versa.

When I started my blog I was delighted to find one day that a lot of traffic seemed to be coming my way from a website called Innovative Passive Income. I saw that Cameron Rogers, who was on the other side of the world, had created links to my website from his site and had contributed to my website by posting constructive comments. This was my first taste of how lovely the blogging community is and how there is plenty of room for anyone who is actively giving value. I subscribed to his website and found lots of great information that was useful in my business. In my experience there is plenty of room for new people to come into an established market if you are providing something of value.

Analysing your visitors' behaviour

Once you have designed and implemented your plan for regular new content, monitor the behaviour of your website visitors with a tool such as Google Analytics. Google Analytics is a free application that you can embed into your website to collect data about your visitors, your traffic sources, popular keywords, your most popular content and much more. This is an essential tool for every website as you can see what impact your developments are having, including spikes in visitors, noticing when people come from a new source, understanding what your visitors consider most valuable and seeing which of your articles they didn't appreciate!

Understanding the behaviour of your website visitors is essential so that you can measure what works and what doesn't work in your quest for growth, and this is one application that you must become familiar with if you are serious about creating a successful internet business. Using an analytics tool will give you instant feedback on the actions you are taking and help you direct your efforts in growing the business. Use it from the moment your website is up.

 Case study: Grassroots Internet Strategy

At Grassroots, the first product we created was an eCourse called Step-by-Step Website Planning for Start-Ups. We put 15 years of combined knowledge and experience into the eBook—it was everything we wanted to share with first-time website builders.

There was a point nearing its completion when we started to become nervous. It had taken us years and years to learn this and we were combining it all into one eCourse and selling it for less than $100! Were we going to do ourselves out of business?

We soon realised, however, that it was our opportunity to provide information and a valuable service to a massive group of people and solve a lot of pain and suffering. What happened was that the product cemented our relationship with our customers and brought ongoing opportunities which were to be of value and generate revenue.

From sharing everything with our consumers the subscription rates to our blogs increased significantly and we realised that people would buy our future products because they received value from the previous one. Worrying about giving too much information was small-minded. We realised that we needed to have a big, long-term vision for the business and provide immense value at every opportunity.

The value of your business is in your database

Your database of current and potential clients is one of your biggest assets; aim to grow it quickly and continuously. This is often overlooked in the quest for sales and sales leads, but data collection is essential because if you have a person's contact information and they subscribe to your emails, you can sell to them again and again (and again). If you have a database that is steadily growing, you have an increasing pool of people who are interested in what you are doing and saying. Through that resource you can generate revenue. It is far better to have 500 people in your database who are really happy to receive your emails than 5000 visitors a month who visit once and never return.

People often need to receive communications from you a number of times before they will make a purchase. Having the contact details of people in your target audience allows you to send different offers, content and messages on an ongoing basis, each aimed at moving them closer to being ready to buy, be willing to buy from time to time or follow links to those things you recommend.

Building a database

When people visit your website, it is much easier for them to decide to 'sign up' for something (particularly if it is quick and easy) than make a decision that involves spending money. So, create a real reason for your visitors to subscribe to your database; give them something they can't refuse.

When the aim is to collect data and build a list for email marketing, keep the information you request to a minimum, such as asking for their name and email address. If you need more, ask for it, but keep in mind that the more information you request, the more likely it is that people will exit before finishing the sign-up process. Less is definitely more.

Put your calls to action to subscribe in a prominent place on your website — like the right-hand corner of your header or in the top of your side column and at the end of each article.

Here are six ways to motivate your website visitors to give you their contact details.

Product/service samples

Ian Hunter runs a dance studio called Logan Dance Sydney. On his website he offers a free lesson in a group class to anyone who signs up to the site. It is a great incentive to subscribe for anyone considering classes, and once they try the classes they generally love them and stay. If you provide services, this is a good way to not only have people subscribe but also to have them come and try out your business.

Competitions

People respond well to competitions when they can win prizes that would be of value to them. Find sponsors who would benefit from the promotion to give you free products that you can give away to the winners. As we discussed earlier, when seeking sponsors choose products and services that would appeal to your target community.

Newsletters

A popular way to build your database is by asking your web visitors to subscribe to your newsletter so you can keep them up to date about what you are doing. The number of subscriptions you get will relate to the perceived value of the information that you have to share. Let people know how frequently you will send the newsletter and only send high-quality content. Newsletters are a great way of periodically communicating with your database. However, with the information overload that so many of us experience, the offer of a newsletter might not be a sufficient incentive for people to give you their details and you may need to consider using this strategy in conjunction with another.

Blog updates

If your blog is useful to people they will want to subscribe to receive future posts. Let them know the frequency of your blog and what they can expect from you. Some companies send blogs every few hours and some may do a weekly round-up. As in relation to newsletters, the offer of a regular blog might not be a sufficient incentive for people to give you their contact details, so use it in conjunction with another strategy.

For example, Philippa Lowe runs Publicity Express and helps small business owners do their own PR. She offers weekly posts of PR tips as well as a *Publicity Secrets Report* when new people subscribe.

Free eBooks

You can provide huge value with free eBooks on topics that would interest your readers. You can either purchase a licence for an existing eBook, have someone write one for you or write your own. For example, at Grassroots we provide a free eBook called *Top 11 Website Mistakes and How to Avoid Them*. Feedback indicates that our readers find the content useful and it continues to give us a significant number of subscriptions. Free eBooks are a great way to collect personal data and it's also a really good way to get known by people early on and to establish your value. Remember though—even though you are providing something for free, it is important that you make sure it is a quality product that represents you well. Give them a great taste of your future paid products.

Free web seminars

Get an expert (it could be you) to deliver a web seminar on a particular topic. They are a great opportunity to interact with people and be a personality. People like to see the real person behind your website. Even if you get another subject matter expert to speak, it is a format that gives depth to your offering. There is no reason why you can't charge for web seminars as well, but free ones can be used to establish yourself and encourage subscriptions. Promote the event, use a good webinar facility and get a USB headset (good sound quality is essential). These can be aired live, and if you record the sessions you will have a great video or audio file that you can use for other purposes as well.

Social media networks

As well as the database you collect on your website, you can also collect social media databases by creating networks on sites such as Facebook, LinkedIn and Twitter. Although you will not have access to email addresses, these networking sites will allow you to connect with and update people on a regular basis in a personal way. So make the most of these networks in the same way that you do your main database—give them value and be consistent. These types of databases can have huge value *in addition* to your email database, but at the end of the day your well-kept email database will be your biggest asset.

The wrap-up

➪ Although some forms of income generation are obvious when you visit a website, it is important to understand the big picture of how money goes around online and the options available to you.

➪ When developing your own income-generating strategies, take a multi-faceted approach as some things will work well for you and some things won't.

➪ It takes time to learn how to implement each strategy well, so be patient and test everything thoroughly.

➪ The key to website success is to give value. Start to evaluate the websites you visit daily; recognise what you find valuable so that you can emulate it on your own website.

➪ You can provide value in any form, including information, entertainment, inspiration and opportunities. The key to giving value is consistency and quality.

➥ Make sure you are measuring your visitors' behaviour so that you can judge their reactions to your content.

➥ Build a database—as fast as you can. A loyal, good-sized database is your biggest asset in the income-generation game. Think of an incentive that your visitors can't refuse.

➥ In addition to your email database you can create databases using social media forums such as Twitter and Facebook. These are great additions to your email database but they do not replace it.

How to sell yourself online

While you may have an absolutely brilliant idea, unless you know how to sell it on the internet it will remain just a good idea.

In this chapter we will look at:

➾ how to build an online personality, including choosing a domain name

➾ the essential elements for an internet business

➾ top tips for website marketing.

Create your website personality

As you will not physically be present on your website, you need to create an online personality synonymous with your style of content and the products or services you are offering. To do this you need to create a great name and domain name.

Choosing a name

Choose a name for your website, business or personality that you really like and that you will be happy to say, use and be associated with. One of the keys is for it to be easy to remember and easy to spell. It does not have to relate to who you are as a company or person, but should be related to the industry, sector or theme of the content and services you are offering. Brainstorm names for your website; go wild—this is what will define you.

Two of my favourite website names are Man vs Debt and Sober Paddy. Man vs Debt documents the adventures of Adam, his wife Courtney and their young daughter Milligan after packing and selling up their life, paying off their debts and choosing a life of adventure and travel instead. Sober Paddy documents the trials and tribulations of an Irishman's decision to stop drinking alcohol. Both of these names conjure up images that not only describe the blog topic perfectly but they are funny, catchy and memorable.

When you have found one you like, see if the name is taken as a domain name and as a trading name. You need to avoid using a name that is protected by a trademark or other registration; your tax office or government business registry will have a list of business names that you can check against.

In this day and age finding an available domain name that suits your business name can sometimes be a creative process, so be prepared to vary the domain name a little as someone may already have the one you want.

To help you think of possible names, start to think of the personality you want your website to have. Your website personality is the shop front of your business and is made up of a voice, a particular look and feel, a style of content and so on. Think then about a name that reflects this. Think how you can play on words. Put words together and think about how you can make your name stand out from the crowd. Think also about words that people will commonly and easily associate with your website and what you're doing.

Consider that you will use the name over and over again, possibly for years—so make sure you like it! Have fun but don't try to be too clever; your name needs to be clear, accessible, repeatable and searchable the world over.

Domain name extensions

When choosing a domain name you will also have a selection of domain extensions to choose from. Consider the following:

➥ If your target consumers are global or in the US, try to choose a .com.

➥ If your target consumers are country-specific, choose your appropriate country extension such as .co.nz in New Zealand, .com.au in Australia or .co.uk in the UK.

Once you have selected a name, write it down and make sure it looks good as a domain, is easy to read and easy to spell. Remember—make it easy for people to find and remember you!

Registering your domain name

There are hundreds of domain name websites that will let you search to see if your preferred domain name is available. I use Cheap Australian Domains, who are well priced and, despite the name, sell domain extensions for most countries.

To check the availability of the name you want, go to <www.cheapaustraliandomains.com.au>, enter your suggested name in the domain name search field, check that the extension boxes are ticked for your preference (such as .com or .co.uk) and click Go!

This will bring up a list showing the availability of your name. If your name is available you are in business. If not, go back and repeat the process with variations until you have an available domain name that you are happy with.

To register your domain name you will need to set up an account. Domain names vary in cost depending on the extension, with .com being the cheapest from $9 to $19 per year.

Note: if you want to buy a .com.au name you will need an Australian business number (ABN). If you do not have one you can register for one free at <www.abr.gov.au>.

Your domain name is hugely important so make sure you don't let it expire, as someone else may take ownership and all of your marketing efforts and hard work will be in vain.

Seven website essentials

In this section we will look at the seven key ingredients for creating a revenue-generating website. The idea is that you get the basics up quickly so that you can focus on the real work, which is to attract visitors, turn visitors into subscribers and turn subscribers into customers.

A good content-driven website is something that evolves over time; it is never 'finished'. For this reason, if you are new to the game the objective is to start somewhere and then improve and develop as you go. Most people find that after six to twelve months they have outgrown their first website because they can see everything they need that they didn't know to think of when they started! With this in mind, take the quickest and easiest entry point into having a revenue-generating website and then upgrade it once you have some experience in managing it and knowing what you want and what you're doing.

Content management system

A content management system, or CMS, is exactly as it sounds: a system that manages your website content. It is the functional part of your website that, at the very least, allows you to update the pages and posts on your website. It is absolutely essential that you have access to your content management system as you need to be able to update your website daily if necessary. You do not want to have to rely on another person to look after the updating for you; it can be frustrating, limiting and costly.

There are several different types of content management systems. If you are starting out with a blog-based website I recommend WordPress. It is a free, open source blogging app-lication that can be customised to meet your needs.

There are two versions: Wordpress.com and Wordpress.org. Wordpress.org is sometimes a little fiddly to install but far more useful and customisable. If you are serious about selling something, definitely go for the .org version. If you are a little technically minded, you can do it yourself with some help from Google, or better still use a host such as HostGator that has its own auto installer.

Design and layout

Most people focus exclusively on the look and feel of their web-site, not realising that it is equally, if not more, important to focus on a layout that is designed for sales flow and functionality. I'm not suggesting that you don't have an aesthetically fabulous website; however, it is more important to have a website that compels your visitors to take action and subscribe or buy.

If you are using Wordpress.org there are hundreds of good-looking themes that you can use. You have a choice from a huge variety of free themes or premium themes that cost up to $100. Do a Google search and take some time to go through lots of themes until you find something you like that will work for the type of content you have. Installing themes is straightforward, so if you like a few free ones download them all to try on your website once it is up.

For the purposes of a blog, you want your website to be easy to read and easy to navigate, with good clear titles and headers. If your content is predominantly text, then black writing on a white background is by far the easiest to read. In terms of website layout, in particular for blogs that are all about content, keep it simple and have your content presented in clear fonts.

Website copy

The copy on your website is all the written content, including everything that tells people who you are, what you do and what you want them to do—such as subscribe or buy. For a blog, much of your written content is delivered in the form of blogs and so your copy is something you will update regularly. You also need to think about some static pages, such as 'About us' and 'Contacts', from the beginning.

Professional website copywriting is an art form that takes into account keywords for optimising the website and the fact that people may either read word for word or skim through the text. So consider learning more or hiring someone once you have products to sell.

Make sure you proofread and spell check your copy before you post it; it always helps to have someone with a fresh pair of eyes proof it for you for grammar, logic and context. A good way to test the flow of any written material you post on your website is to read it out loud.

Hosting

A website hosting company does exactly what it says—they host your website on the internet. Your website is a set of files that needs to be accessible every time someone types in your website address. The host computer holds your website files ready and available to potential visitors 24 hours a day. There are many different packages ranging from $0 to $50 or more per month, so shop around. Blogs do not require much data transfer, so go with a hosting package that is cheap and flexible, such as HostGator. HostGator is affordable, hosts hundreds of thousands of blogs and offers great support. They also have additional features that make installing WordPress quick and easy.

Subscription and incentives

As I mentioned in the previous chapter, building a database of contacts is extremely important for the growth and success of your website. The best way to manage this is with an email marketing service. These range from $0 to $100 or more per month. It is essential to use an email marketing service that looks after:

⇨ managing the subscription and un-subscription process

⇨ the production of professional-looking html or plain text emails

⇨ reporting and tracking of user behaviour.

An email marketing service automates your subscriptions both on your website and in your newsletters and emails. MailChimp is the best email marketing service I have come across for small business website owners, and it is free if you have fewer than 2000 subscribers. You can customise headers, colour schemes and fonts, and the bottom of your emails are designed with everything required to have you comply with regulations for email marketing.

MailChimp reports on the behaviour of your readers and you can customise your emails and newsletters. You can also use it for distribution of free eBooks and documents, and it has a free WordPress plugin that embeds a sign-up form on your website.

As well as all these features, the most important reason why you should use an email marketing service is that they are set up to help you avoid having your email address blacklisted (by removing email addresses that bounce, among other things) and so that your emails comply with anti-spam laws.

Payment applications

If you are selling something on your website you will need a means of accepting payments. The most widely used service is currently PayPal. Services such as PayPal charge you a percentage of each transaction, which is great for a small start-up website because you have no monthly overheads; you only pay as you generate revenue.

PayPal does not do everything, however, and so another application to add to the mix is one that helps you manage the tracking of your sales, distribution of products and affiliate program. E-Junkie looks after everything that PayPal doesn't cover, as well as being an affiliate marketplace. You can also use E-Junkie as a distribution point if you sell products on ClickBank. At $5 per month it is an extremely useful and cost-effective tool for your online business.

Again I recommend you keep it simple and flexible; you will always have the opportunity in the future to invest in custom options. With so many cost-effective, purpose-built applications available, only invest in custom options once you have some experience in running your website and can see its limitations.

Affiliate programs

If you are selling products on your website, you may as well have other people promoting them for you too! Some people baulk at the thought of giving away a percentage of the sales price, but in the digital world a good affiliate program can help you sell significantly more. Think of affiliates as your team of commission-only salespeople who you don't even have to meet or interview! They will just do their sales thing promoting your products, and you only pay them once they have made you some money. In return they get to jump on the product bandwagon and make a percentage of sales from your lovely products … sound good?

You will find that a small portion of your affiliates make most of the sales so look after them, and be easy to contact for questions and suggestions. Use E-Junkie to create your own affiliate program or register with ClickBank to take advantage of their marketplace. ClickBank will manage payments to all parties, including reconciling payments for returns.

As you can see there are a lot of 'behind the scenes' applications and services needed to create a successful revenue-generating website. What I have talked about are a collection of services that you can simply register for and use with very little technical knowledge. This set up will get you into the marketplace with little cost and development needed.

There is absolutely nothing wrong with investing in purpose-designed websites down the track which will incorporate many of the functions of these applications, but if you are following a blog-based website model this is a good low-cost entry into the market while you explore the world of internet marketing. For some people this will be all you ever need to happily manage a successful web business.

Nine great ways to market your website

Your ability to succeed with your business will rely heavily on you being found by your target market. There are millions of websites out there so you will need to spend a large proportion of your business time on marketing. There are a lot of very effective —and very ineffective—ways of marketing your website. I have included nine methods here that are really working for me, and some examples of how you can make the most of each one.

Social media marketing

Social media marketing, or SMM, is my favourite type of marketing and uses social networks for marketing, sales, public relations and customer service. Used successfully, SMM applications such as Twitter, Facebook and LinkedIn will let you communicate with customers and potential customers and build a community around your business.

These applications can add powerful visibility to you and your products or services, and used well can bring warm visitors to your website. The key to social media marketing is to understand how each audience interacts with the application so that you create marketing that does not conflict with the culture of the environment. So take some time when you first get involved to understand how people interact and what the etiquette is.

Even if your only intention is to use the application to increase the number of visitors to your website, you need to understand how people use it at a personal level so that you can craft your approach to suit the 'natives'. For example, when people are using Facebook they are there for social reasons and they are generally friends with the people they interact with. It is intimate and informal, which means the tone of postings is warm and fuzzy and about self-expression. Remember that when you send messages, and post for people with that mindset. If your messages are formal and 'salesy' they will stick out and will probably be received with contempt.

It is also important that your posts send a consistent message. Social media allows you to demonstrate the personality of your website so choose your communications carefully. Create relevant posts, be personable, fun, friendly and easy to approach, and most importantly give value, whether it be inspiration, information or entertainment.

Like your subscription database, people who subscribe to you through social media networks are interested in getting regular information from you. It is easier to get someone to subscribe to you on Facebook or Twitter because they generally just have to click a 'like' or 'follow' button rather than entering their contact details into a form, so use this to benefit your website.

With social media you can listen to what is happening in your industry and with your potential customers. Get involved in conversations and be a dynamic person rather than just a company front. When you see anything cool or useful related to your industry, post it. If you produce new content, link to it. Use it to make and maintain business friendships the same way you would personal friendships and networks, by being interested, interesting and involved.

Content marketing

As its name suggests, content marketing is when you use content to attract people to your website, products or services. There are several ways of doing this.

Writing blogs and articles

Your blogs and articles are the lifeblood of your website. But you can use them elsewhere as well. After posting your articles on your website, link to them on your Facebook and Twitter and repurpose them to use on external websites. EzineArticles, for example, allows you to post articles along with biographical data about the author. The bonus is that these articles may show up independently in Google for particular keywords, and when people are looking for content they can use your article (in its entirety) on their site, which includes your bio and links to your website.

Guest blogging

This is the art of preparing articles specifically for someone else's website. Look for websites that have a similar target market to you, ask them if you can guest blog, and make some suggestions on what you can offer that would benefit their readers. If they say yes, create a good-quality article that is designed specifically for them. Make sure you have a clear, concise bio at the bottom of the blog that links to your website.

The bigger the database and readership of the website you are guest blogging for, the more beneficial it will be for your business. Many websites today collate blogs and articles from various external sources, each one presenting an opportunity to increase awareness about your work and your value in the industry.

Writing reviews

Writing reviews works in a similar way to writing articles. The added bonus is that if someone happens to be looking on Google for the product you have reviewed, there is a chance, depending on how competitive the keywords are, that your website will be presented in the organic listings. If you find a really good and relevant product or service, or attend a great industry event, write a review about it. If you are registered for the affiliate program for the product, make sure you include the links. If people are inspired to purchase a product or service because of a review you wrote, you have the opportunity to make a commission.

There are laws in some countries regulating transparency for the promotion of affiliate products, so make sure you comply. I believe, however, that regardless of the rules it is worth disclosing affiliate links because you want your community to feel that there is no trickery. It's important that your community and followers feel they can trust you.

Video blogs

A fantastic way to diversify how you communicate with your audience is with video blogs. If you do them in one take, it is quicker than the time it takes to write a blog, They show the world who you are and allow people to get to know you in a different, more personal way. You become 'real' for people. Add video and audio to your posts and you will keep all your visual and auditory types happy too.

Use YouTube to host your video blogs. YouTube is an authority site, which means that videos posted rank highly in Google search results. The benefit is that you will sometimes find your YouTube videos show up in the organic listings in Google within days, when it can take weeks or months (or more) for your website to show up for the same search terms.

Case studies and testimonials

Good testimonials add personality and foster the credibility of your website, products and services. Case studies and test-imonials should be included in the plan for any website. Once people know you provide the services or products they are looking for, they will want to make sure you are a quality supplier. As well as your articles and 'About us' page, testimonials are often read when judging whether to contact a company or purchase products online. For this reason it is important to have great testimonials and customer feedback easily found on your website.

Make sure your testimonials are:

➭ *Positive*. Of course!

➭ *Specific to a product or service*. When you ask for testimonials, be specific about the product or service that you want the person to comment on, otherwise people will often write general ones.

➭ *Honest*. Keep it real! If your testimonials are too good to be true they will be seen that way. Keep the essence and personality of each person who writes them.

➭ *Credible*. Include the name, position and company name of the person who gave the testimonial. If you can include a photo of the person, do it, and if you can have them agree to do a video testimonial pat yourself on the back!

➭ *Succinct*. While you want some good detail, avoid producing a novel.

➭ *Real*. Don't fake them, don't fake them, and really, don't fake them!

Email marketing

Email marketing involves sending an email to a list of recipients for marketing purposes, such as promoting an offer, newsletter, blog, event or new article. Email campaigns are a cost-effective way of sharing information with your database, and encouraging traffic back to your website. To build an email marketing plan you'll need:

➭ email marketing software

➭ an email design template that is consistent with your website image and branding

➭ a method of tracking the results of your campaigns, including how many people opened the email and clicked on the links, and ideally any returns from the campaign, such as sales generated

✎ a plan for how frequently you will send your emails

✎ an idea of the type of content that your subscribers will find of value.

The first three can be covered by an application such as Mail-Chimp, as can your subscription process.

Email marketing basics include automatically posting your regular blogs to your database. As with everything the key is quality and consistency.

Search engine optimisation and building links

Lots of people get freaked out by the term search engine opti-misation (SEO). Don't be. You need to know the basics, which I will give you here, and the rest you can learn as you go (or use an SEO expert). SEO is aimed at increasing your web traffic by having your website appear in organic search results when you search for something in search engines such as Google. Organic search results are those appearing on the left-hand side of a search engine results page. These results are not paid for.

In WordPress there is a great plugin called SEO All in One Pack that helps you put all the right words in the right places in the backend of the website, as well as in every page and post you place on your website. This completely simplifies the process of the basic optimisation of each piece of content you write.

Optimising your website for search engines helps it appear higher in search engine results, making your website visible to more people who search for related products, services and information. This will then translate into more people visiting your website—more traffic. In addition to optimising your website from a content point of view, by including keywords that are based on what people actually search for it can also be optimised from a development point of view by making it search engine friendly. This means it is designed to look good to the search engines, in all the right places! Although no-one outside of Google knows the actual algorithms that they use to judge the value of your website, there are a lot of things that help optimise your website for search engines and improve your search engine rankings, including:

- the number and quality of external links from other websites to yours; the more authoritative the websites that link to you the better

- use of keywords, including in your page titles (also called the title tag) and throughout the content

- size of your website — the more relevant pages and content the better; this will develop over time as you add to the site

- how long your website has existed; the longer you have been around the better.

In addition to making your website search engine friendly, building links with other websites can help direct traffic to your website. There is no right amount, but logic dictates that the more links you have the more opportunities you are providing to direct visitors to your website. This can be done easily and help you network at the same time. Every time you read an interesting blog or article, take a few moments to make a comment or respond to the article. Doing so has several benefits. First, you are making your presence known to the website owners and other readers of the article (so make sure you contribute to their website constructively). Secondly, your website link will accompany your name and people may visit you if your comments interest them or provide something of value.

Search engine marketing

Search engine marketing, or SEM, is where you pay to advertise your website on a search engine results page. In Google, this means appearing in what is called the Ads section. Although it can take time for your website to appear on page one of Google search results through your SEO efforts, using search engine marketing you could potentially be listed there by the end of the day.

Depending on how competitive your industry is and how popular your keywords are, you will pay anywhere from a few cents to several dollars each time someone clicks on your ad. You have control over what you spend as you can set a daily budget, so you can test the waters with some flexibility and without breaking the bank.

Ads appear on the Google results page based on what each person is searching for. This means that you can reach people specifically searching for your product or service. Ads can also be targeted to the geographic area that you work in if you require.

If your website is compelling, search engine marketing can bring you a lot of traffic very quickly. However, unless your website is set up to turn those visitors into customers, you could get very little for your money. Use search engine marketing when you are confident that your sales information is attractive to buyers and when you have a good understanding about monitoring your website. Don't underestimate the skill required to successfully use search engine marketing; there are several things you need to do well, including creating the right ads and creating great sales information. It is worth studying the topic, or finding an expert to set it up for you.

Referrals and partnerships

Well-considered recommendations and referrals can be an extremely powerful way to introduce your business to potential customers. Aim to work with referrers who have a strong relationship with their customers. Partnerships like these allow you to leverage the credibility or brand of another organisation in the industry for the benefit of your product or service—it can bring you great credibility as well as sales leads. A well-structured partnership can give a small start-up business owner the public relations and marketing engine of a major organisation. For a small business the benefits of creating smart partnerships and joint ventures can be *huge*!

Following are some ideas for creating smart partnerships that can increase visitors and sales.

Create bundles

Choose partners who have complementary products and services to yours. Create a bundle of your products and services with theirs and advertise the bundle to both company's databases. Not only will it expand your offering but your new partner will be promoting your offerings on your behalf.

Get referrals

Ask for referrals from other businesses and websites. If they see that your business would be of value to their customers, they may be happy to recommend you on their website, newsletter or in an email. If need be, offer them a commission on all sales generated through their referral—you can manage this with your affiliate program.

Note: ask for personal messages. It is always better to have someone recommend you personally. If someone offers you an ad, ask if they wouldn't mind writing a quick review or recommendation to their database instead.

Give something good

Offer your product or services for another business to give to their database as a gift. This way you look good and they are happy to promote you. As their database comes to you to claim their gift, add them to your database and give them a sample of your wares.

Guest blog

As I outlined above, many website owners are looking for content contributors for their website. If you are good at writing and can effectively articulate a topic that your business specialises in, offer to write an article or guest blog for businesses that have the type of audience that you are looking for. You will start to establish yourself as an expert on the subject, and (of course!) link back to your website from the article.

Public relations

In a nutshell, public relations, or PR, is the management of communication between you and the public. The goal of PR is to increase the amount of communication delivered, so that you get as much exposure as possible. The holy grail of PR is a communication that spreads quickly via the internet or that gets major media exposure.

PR is something that you can definitely think about from the beginning, and there are plenty of things that a small business owner can do to become better known. It is worth thinking about PR from the outset as every little bit helps.

Below are some tips for starting out with basic PR.

➥ *Generate press releases.* A press release is a mini news story that is designed to appeal to an editor or reporter who may wish to write a story on the subject. It's important to distinguish a news story from an ad for your business! One publication published my press release verbatim (this is not unusual for smaller publications) so make sure it is very well written.

   Get familiar with your local press. Understand the types of publications that would be interested in your industry, go to their websites and follow their instructions on how to send them a press release. Most organisations give very specific instructions on how to send a release to them, sometimes via an email and sometimes on a website form. If you are unsure, try calling the target publication, pitch your news story and see if they have any further interest.

➥ *Donate prizes to charities.* If you have something of value you can offer, charities are often looking for prizes and giveaways for their fundraising efforts. See how you can partner them as a sponsor, and feel good at the same time.

➸ *Run seminars or webinars on your website.* Interview someone of note, enrol the help of an industry expert or facilitate the sessions yourself. Consider the community your webinar will benefit and see who you can get involved to help promote it.

➸ *Send information about your website, products and services to radio stations.* Community stations are often keen to interview people who are doing interesting things, and you never know your luck: you may get picked up by a commercial station as well.

➸ *Send a regular newsletter to your database.* Share any exciting things you have coming up in among your articles and news.

➸ *Find local resources that provide callouts from the media.* We use an incredibly useful resource called SourceBottle that lets you know which media outlets are looking for stories in your industry. This service is gold to small business owners!

Networking, events, speaking

An essential way to promote your online business is in the physical world. You can do this through networking and industry events. Find out where and when your industry meets and get involved. Take every opportunity to talk to people and find out what they do. Often at networking events they will give a few people opportunities to speak about their business; jump at the chance, even if you are nervous! Use networking events to find like-minded business owners with complementary services and create partnerships and joint ventures with them.

The most beneficial thing you can do at networking events is get up and present. As you start to establish your credibility in a certain field, grab any and all opportunities to contribute what you know and have learned. This could be anything from a small network in a living room through to presenting to large groups in concert halls. Put yourself out there and these opportunities will start to present themselves.

Forums

Online forums are great for networking and conversing without having to take off your slippers! Find forums that best serve your industry and get involved. Look for conversations that you can contribute to. Post questions and give lots of answers. Be interested and be of value and you will find plenty of opportunities to indirectly promote your website and your expertise.

Many forums allow you to have a signature space where you can include your company links and a brief description of what you do. Make sure you take advantage of that space if it's offered. Also read the terms as they vary from website to website, and you don't want to be removed for inadvertently breaking the rules!

 Case study: Grassroots Internet Strategy

At each step of the way we tried different forms of marketing, with varying results. What can work beautifully for one business may not work for another. Most things take a little time to get used to while learning how to be effective.

Our social media marketing has consisted of a Twitter account, a Facebook group, a LinkedIn group and more recently a Facebook page. Approximately 30 per cent of our website traffic comes from social media, and we like the personal interaction we have with our followers, friends and *likes*.

Content marketing is one of our core strategies; we post blogs every week covering all manner of useful tips and articles that would be of value to our readers, and then send them to our email and RSS subscribers as well as to our social networks. From time to time we repurpose them for e-zine articles which gives us additional visitors to the website. Mel also guest blogs on other sites from time to time and we send out monthly newsletters.

For search engine optimisation we have optimised the website for our keyword phrases and use the SEO All in One Pack plugin in WordPress that has handy fields to populate all the right places. We also use the same plugin on every page and post, and we analyse where the traffic is coming from in the search engines using Google Analytics.

Our affiliate marketing program using E-Junkie has grown steadily, and we have just started to take advantage of their marketplace. This allows us to post our products in case someone is looking for exactly what we do. We offer affiliates 50 per cent commission on all product sales they refer to us.

With search engine marketing we pay for small amounts of clicks in Google AdWords. We direct these visitors to specific product pages. We have kept our budget at $5 per day as we work out our sales copy. We started this marketing much later in the piece and it has good potential for growth, but we have not seen the results yet.

For PR, we developed a month-by-month plan for PR activities, including an annual survey of websites related to our field. We held the first survey in 2010 and collected some great data that we can use for press releases and to define our offering. We offer free live webinars once a month so people can get extra help and have access to us personally. This has been a great way to add a personal touch for people who subscribe to our website, and a reason for new people to actively participate and get to know us from the outset. We also apply for appropriate call outs on SourceBottle. Recently this has included three video interviews for industry websites.

We subscribe to a couple of local industry forums, and contribute from time to time answering questions and getting involved in conversations. Through networking we have both been offered

Case study *(cont'd)* : Grassroots Internet Strategy

opportunities to speak to groups of new entrepreneurs and business owners, and this is another area we are just starting to pursue.

Marketing your website is essential to your ability to grow and create revenue streams; the more you spend marketing it the faster you will get the desired result. We schedule in time every week for blog writing and marketing and we try to be as consistent as possible with the limited time we have available.

The wrap-up

- To create your low-maintenance income you need to have a website that works and you need to understand where to put your efforts to market it.

- Choose a website personality that you could love for years to come and a name that is easy for people to remember.

- It is critical that you have access to your content management system so that you can make changes to the website as quickly and often as you need to.

- The design and layout should present your content and calls to action so that they are compelling and easy to read.

- Give people a great reason to subscribe—an offer they can't refuse!

- Your affiliate program will give people the opportunity to earn commissions for promoting you which is beneficial to you and them.

- Social media marketing such as Twitter and Facebook are a great way to get personal with customers and potential customers.

▷ Use good email marketing software to make sure that your emails meet regulatory standards.

▷ Leverage other people's businesses and databases with referrals and partnerships. Be smart and offer something great that will benefit both businesses.

▷ Making the most of public relations is important even if you are a one-man or one-woman band.

▷ Offline marketing such as networking and speaking to groups will grow your network and the strength of your network exponentially.

Chapter 7

Creating your own products

Affiliate marketing gives you plenty of opportunities to profit from other people's products and you should start this type of revenue generation from the outset. However, once your website is developing and your database is growing it is time to consider producing your own digital products (if you don't already). Creating your own products will help you to establish your expertise and add to your opportunities for creating revenue. They give a marketplace of potential affiliates a reason to promote you.

The success of any product comes down to your ability to attractively package great content while making it accessible and compelling to your target audience. If your product is amazing but no-one knows about it, it won't be a huge success. Similarly, it doesn't matter how great your product is if the sales information you provide is boring or uninformative.

The first questions you must answer are: what product should you create? Where should you start?

There are many factors to consider when choosing what product to create, and during the product development process. The following takes you through some creative and technical processes that will help you identify topics that will work for your community and how to transform your ideas into various tangible products you can sell.

Throughout this chapter I will primarily discuss writing an eBook, however I will also show you other types of digital products you can create.

What is it for?

First things first — before you start production, be clear about what your product is for. It is important to know what outcome you want before you start. The two main outcomes you can aim for are collecting subscriptions and generating income. Both cases provide an opportunity to establish your expertise.

Collecting subscriptions

This is a great place to start. Create a valuable product that you will give away for free to people who subscribe to your database. A free eBook can be as short or as long as you want. The important thing is that it really represents your work well and will provide value to those who receive it. Free products must be:

- on a topic that will attract the right types of subscribers
- valuable or useful
- easy to access
- a good representation of other work you may produce (written using the same 'voice')
- distributed automatically
- able to create other opportunities for your business.

Generating income

Products that you will sell need to be of great quality and value to your customers. Think about topics that would be really helpful to your community that won't lose relevance over time. While it is standard practice to make updates to digital products, it is best not to choose topics that will become obsolete after a couple of years.

When creating products for sale it is important that they are:

⇨ high quality

⇨ well edited and tested by people in the target market

⇨ professionally presented

⇨ designed for longevity

⇨ easily distributed.

With all of these goals it is important that you objectively analyse your progress as you sharpen your skills in internet marketing. Don't be disheartened by slow sales or subscriptions at first; it is all part of the process of establishing your business.

What is it about?

When choosing a topic for your product it is important to consider the people you have ready access to, including your visitors, your subscribers and any partnerships or groups that you can leverage.

With your visitors and subscribers, you are already developing a relationship with them because they are consuming what is already on your website. They get something from your communications, whether it is information, entertainment, inspiration or opportunities. So don't let them down! When choosing what you are going to produce, consider very carefully a product that would appeal to the same group of people. Ask yourself these questions:

⇨ What are my visitors interested in when they visit my website?

☞ What are the types of challenges that they face?

☞ What do I help them with?

☞ Which blog topics were the most popular on my website?

☞ Are there any questions that come up often in the industry or in comments or emails sent by readers?

☞ What would I love to share?

The answers to these questions will start to give you some potential topics for your product. If you have a lot of ideas, start with your favourite one (yes, listen to your gut!) as you can always produce other products later.

The digital products with the best chance of success are the ones that solve a need, help people to make something easier or show them how they can succeed at something. So think about solutions to the problems that people face in your community.

Business partnerships

Look out for opportunities to work in a partnership with another complementary business. Glenn Murray's business, Divine Write, specialises in SEO copywriting. One day at a conference he met one of the speakers, Darren Rowse, who is the founder of ProBlogger, a blog about professional blogging. They realised they possessed complementary skills and resources, and decided to collaborate on an eBook to help bloggers write great posts: *The Copywriting Scorecard for Bloggers*. The eBook was produced as a collaborative effort, and the marketing was a joint effort. Joining forces resulted in a better book, extended reach and increased profitability.

How to produce a great product (even if you hate writing)

Once you are clear about what you want to achieve with your product and who you are creating it for, you need to think about production. There are several important aspects to address, such as your voice, the structure and the appropriateness of your product for your audience.

The style and personality of your product

It is critical that you translate the style and personality you developed for your website into your product. If you've followed the process I set out in earlier chapters, people will be familiar with receiving communications from you that will look, read and sound a certain way. The style of the content you have provided so far will be familiar to them, so it is important to be consistent with your products and make sure the same voice shines through.

As well as thinking about the content, it is important to think about the presentation of your product. For eBooks and eCourses think about adding pictures, videos or graphs for example. Use clear, readable fonts, clear, bold headers, a title page and a table of contents. Consider colour schemes and how the text is positioned on each page. With eBooks, many of your customers will be reading them on a computer screen and so it is okay to use a bigger font with good spacing. Also, unless you have a really good reason not to, make sure your background is white, which is easier to read and doesn't cost your customers in unnecessary ink if they print your book.

When your product is ready, decide if it looks professional enough to match the value you are placing on the product; if you are not confident that it does, employ a graphic designer to create a look and feel that works with your branding. Also, importantly, get the designer to design an image that is a visual representation of the product for use in sales pages and ads on websites.

Who will write it?

For written products, if you dislike writing or just don't have the time, ask someone to write it for you. While many people find the idea of writing their first book exciting or have dreamed of writing and publishing a piece of work, for some the idea is simply daunting. If this is you, you are in luck; there is a huge industry of people who will co-author or ghost write your book.

Co-authoring is where someone shares the task of developing the content and you are jointly credited as authors. Co-authoring will generally come as an opportunity based on knowing or meeting someone with complementary skills, as with Glenn and Darren.

Ghost writing is where someone writes on your behalf and you are credited as the author. It is fairly common to produce the ideas, expertise and direction of the book and have a ghost writer collate that into a finished product. Just because you're an expert in your field doesn't make you a good or interesting writer, or you may simply not have the time.

Whether you want a ghost writer to write the whole product for you or you want someone to structure your draft, there are plenty of places you can go to find writers, including Freelance Switch, Elance and oDesk. You can see people's previous work and how much they charge, and offer people the opportunity to work with you. These sites all work slightly differently but the premise is similar; you post your job, interested writers will 'bid' for it and you can select your freelancer.

Use social media such as Facebook, Twitter or LinkedIn to ask your network for recommendations as well. I have created many business opportunities and partnerships (including Grass-roots Internet Strategy!) from posting on Facebook or Twitter.

Regardless of the extent of your or their involvement, it's important that you are involved in the whole process and are happy with the result as it's being produced. If you are co-authoring a product, make sure you agree in advance about how you will tackle differences of opinion about the content and that you settle on a voice and style you are both happy with. If the product will be credited in your name but you do not write it, make sure it reflects who you are as a person, and your business. More often than not, you will need to do some editing (as nobody thinks quite like you), so make sure you keep that in mind and set aside sufficient time to go through that process.

Make it accessible

It is important that your product is easy to consume and doesn't alienate people because it is difficult to comprehend. It's important to understand your target market; unless you are designing it specifically for an intellectual market, ensure that you write or speak in language that is accessible for people with varying reading and comprehension levels.

If you must use jargon, explain it, and if you think that novices in your industry may purchase your product then provide them with plenty of explanation. This may be in the body of the work or in attached documents or reference sheets. Remember you can include as many documents as you like as part of your product, which is one of the benefits of digital products.

Use examples as often as you can to illustrate what you're talking about, and keep it simple, succinct and tight. Don't get unnecessarily technical as your key messages will be lost and so will your readers.

It is important to create and maintain structure. List the key points you want to articulate, and then expand those into a paragraph and then into a chapter. If you are producing a video product, create clear points and then summarise them at the end.

Basically, do anything you can to make your product as easy to consume and understand as possible. When you have finished the first draft, it is worth considering different people's perspectives, so ask people who know little or nothing about the subject to review it and give you feedback.

Three formulae for producing useful products

The structure of your product will dictate who you need to get involved in developing it. Here are some suggestions for some commonly used formulae that you can use to produce a valuable digital product.

Expert panel formula

The expert panel formula is where a number of experts contribute their expertise on a particular topic. These contributions are collated and form the basis of your product. This has four main benefits:

➦ Most of the content is produced by other people, which means less work for you!

➦ You are acknowledging your experts as experts and are offering them a chance to be promoted to your database, community and future consumers of your product.

➦ If each of your expert panel promotes your product you massively increase your marketing power and the reach of your product. This will benefit everyone involved.

➦ If your experts are well known their names will bring credibility to your product. This is particularly helpful when you are new to a field and few people know who you are.

Who you choose for your expert panel will depend on your industry, the topic and the contacts you have. Lorraine Cuadro's website The Essence of Breastfeeding, for example, provides breastfeeding advice to new mums and their families. Using the expert panel formula she created a series of audio interviews that she recorded with parenting experts, which were designed to give parents practical information and inspiration on topics such as bullying and confidence building. Lorraine offers this series on her website as a bonus for subscribers.

Before you contact people who could comprise your expert panel, consider how you want them to respond and what expectations you have of them, including the time frame in which you want them to provide their responses or be interviewed, and if you have any expectations of them in regards to marketing. The easier you make the process, the more likely they are to say yes!

You have several options for capturing their responses, such as in writing or by video or audio interview. For an eBook, for example, email them the questions and have them respond. You could ask each expert the same questions, craft separate questions or ask them to write a specific section or chapter of the eBook.

It helps if you get experts who specialise in different parts of the same topic; for example, if you had a health-related blog, you could ask a GP, a naturopath, a chiropractor, a personal trainer and an energy healer to each give their perspective on a certain topic. If your blog relates to helping bands become known in the music industry, you could do a video interview with someone from a recording studio, a distribution company, a radio station, a booking agency and a record label, with tips on how to best position a band to be noticed by their company. Then package the videos as a series or edit them together.

I've found it pays to ask more people than I need. If you want five respondents, try asking seven. Even if they all say yes, the reality is that most people (especially experts!) are busy, so make sure you are covered in case some don't deliver what you want or don't deliver in time.

Top tips formula

The top tips formula is where you provide your top tips on a given subject. This is a commonly used formula for digital products. Once you have chosen your topic, consider all of your top tips, the most useful and helpful things you can think of, the types of things that you either learned successfully or the hard way. Top tips can be very useful to someone new in the industry, and can therefore create a valuable product.

Each of your top tips can become a chapter or section heading that you can then go into in more detail. As with the expert panel formula, there are plenty of ways to deliver this. Jessica Van Den, for example, helps people in the craft industry get online and teaches them how to create income from their crafts. Using the top tips formula she created *Five Ways to Increase Profits with Your Online Craft Biz* on her self-titled blog. She offers consumers two choices: either they subscribe for the tips in the form of a free weekly email for five weeks, or they pay a small fee to download the tips in eBook form at the outset.

Step-by-step guides

If you have technical nous and can impart your knowledge clearly and in great detail, a step-by-step guide may be a good choice for your product. Step-by-step guides can take away much of the difficultly, frustration and wasted time of learning something new, and people will search these out to avoid the pain of the unknown.

With such guides, keep your language simple and jargon free, and if appropriate include plenty of diagrams and visual representations of what you are teaching. If you are teaching something that is accessed on a computer, for example, take lots of screen shots so that you can show the steps you want people to take, or use a screen and audio recorder to record and attach video of the demonstrations.

Your guide can be delivered in any form—with eCourse, eBook and video being the most common—or in a combination of media types.

Make sure you get plenty of people to test and review your guides, and only put them on the market once you are happy that they are clear, accurate and simple enough for your target customers to understand and follow.

Case study: Grassroots Internet Strategy

Our first eBook was called *Top 11 Website Mistakes and How to Avoid Them*. It is a four-page eBook using the top tips formula, and we give it away free. It is short, sharp and pithy, and has proved to be really useful to people looking for that kind of information. In addition to this we offer a free web seminar on the same topic every month for people who have more questions or prefer a more interactive approach.

With the eBook we knew exactly what we wanted to write, and it took us about 10 hours each to develop the information.

Our paid products are much more detailed and sophisticated. We have produced a few eCourses that have taken 100 to 200 hours each to prepare and are between 30 and 60 pages, plus additional resources. With the paid products we paid for a template to be designed so that our products look really professional, are easy to read and have a consistent look and feel. Some of our eCourses are made up of several documents and worksheets that come as a zip file.

We co-wrote our *Twitter for Business* eBook and share the profits. Melinda knew Andrea Rotondi, a social media specialist who agreed to write and collate the eBook with her knowledge coupled with content that we had already written.

How will you package your information?

As this book focuses on internet-based businesses, I focus on digital products. Digital products are those that can be down-loaded from the internet — they are not physical.

The benefits of producing digital products are:

⇨ no manufacturing costs

🖎 no shipping costs

🖎 no need to set up a physical shop front

🖎 you do not need to invest in or store unsold stock.

How you package your product depends on your personal preference. Some people may package the same information in more than one form. If, for example, you record an audio series, you can also transcribe the audio to compile as an eBook.

Here are some of the most common types of digital products, and tips for making the most of each.

eBooks

eBooks are similar to a paperback but in digital format. They can be easily updated, and easily distributed. Some people include links to video or audio files. These can be produced and distributed in simple Microsoft Word converted to Adobe Acrobat PDF format, or through more professional and complex applications such as Flash book readers that simulate the book experience with turning pages. When deciding on the format you wish to produce your product in, consider the computer and mobile facilities that your audience will likely have available to them and how you wish to protect the integrity of your product.

Saving your file to PDF will provide a reasonable level of security against people tampering with your product, and the format is widely used. If you are using E-Junkie for distribution, you can stamp the buyer's name, email address and transaction ID on each page of the PDF before they download it, which is a subtle way to discourage buyers from sharing your product.

eBooks can be read on a computer, on mobile phones, on an iPad or similar device, or on dedicated eBook readers such as the Amazon Kindle. Different devices and software accept different file formats, so investigate how you think your product will be used and choose an appropriate file format.

eCourses

eCourses are loosely defined and can be anything from simple how-to guides to interactive live events. They may be provided in PDF form like eBooks, as software applications where people participate in training through your online product or as a download to their computer.

Regardless of the format of your eCourse, be very clear on the outcome you want for people who take the course, and test it thoroughly to be sure that intention is fulfilled. Your eCourse should be clear, step by step, easy to understand, give lots of great tips and provide additional assistance if needed.

You can provide a live element to your eCourse with a webinar or series of webinars. Webinars are internet-based conferences that allow you to present to participants anywhere they can access the internet. There are many webinar facilities available, so shop around for one that fits your budget. When you hold a webinar, you can set the webinar to show your computer screen, so everything you do can be seen by your participants. This way you can show slides or live demonstrations of what you are doing on your computer. Depending on the size of your audience, you can choose to have an open conversation with all of the participants or have them muted when you present. If you record the session, you will also have a video that you can use either as a recap for your course participants or as another product or bonus available to visitors to your website.

Audio products

Audio products include any sort of recorded information, stories or interviews delivered by podcast or audio file. These products are great for people who don't like to write. You can, for example, interview industry gurus, which will give you a very useful product that you can share easily. Alternatively, you can transcribe the interview (or have someone transcribe it for you) for use as an eBook. Use CallBurner to record audio interviews on Skype and your interviewees will not have to leave the comfort of their home.

Collate a series of interviews like you would chapters of a book. If you are interviewing someone, it is often useful to develop the questions you will ask with them as they will likely know what will be of most interest to people. The basic rule is that although it might feel odd at first (especially if you've not done it before), relax and have some fun. People often like to talk about themselves or their passions, which can be really interesting and inspiring—just make sure you manage ramblings and rants from your guests!

Video products

Video is a huge industry, and it gives you a powerful way to interact with your customers in a personal manner that can be used over and over again. Video is accessible, engaging and of course adds a visual element that can be more effective than audio or written work. With the prevalence of free video, it is important that your paid video products stand apart through the quality of production and content.

Laura Snook from Laura Kate Australia produces video workouts. She took her contemporary training style and filmed it against the rugged landscapes of Australia, creating a unique product that is perfectly designed for digital distribution.

Laura uses Flowplayer to distribute the video, which customers can stream or download once they have purchased. Flowplayer is Flash-based, and has a free version which includes their logo or a commercial version that allows you to add your own logo or have no logo at all.

Charlotte from Happyzine created a positive writing course and people could participate through privately shared online training videos. After each video was released the group would then interact with conversations and questions in the group comments area.

It is also common practice for internet marketers to have a DVD product in their offering. To increase the perceived value of a video or set of videos they set up a distribution house to manage the production and delivery of DVD products to order, rather than distributing online.

At the basic level you can use handy tools such as VodBurner to record and edit video interviews through Skype. This can create a great visual interview, easily recorded even when the people involved are in different countries.

Editing your products

Make sure you edit your products thoroughly and frequently so you can be sure that the end product is as good as you can make it. At every stage of the development process have people go through it and critique it. As the product starts taking shape, have a selection of two or three people who are from your target market look at drafts and ask them to give you comprehensive feedback. This is an extremely useful process where you can learn a lot about the perceived value of the structure and content of your product. It's not the time to be precious about your work; be open to constructive criticism in the interests of providing the best offering you can. When you have taken suggested changes and improvements and revised your drafts accordingly, ask another group to review the product. This process can take a while, so—like I said above—make sure you allocate sufficient time to allow for this.

Testimonials and reviews

When your content is nearing completion, think about who you can approach to provide testimonials or reviews. Create a list of people who will benefit most from your product; add to that a list of people in the industry who can lend credibility to your product. Some people will be happy to give you a few words recommending your product if they think it is good. Don't be shy to ask well-known people who are the experts in the space; you never know, they might just say yes!

Pricing

As I discussed in relation to your inherent value, the value of your digital products depends on your confidence in their value and your confidence in the sales process. If you know that the information you are presenting will be immensely valuable then don't undersell yourself. You are better off working on improving your sales process and the value of your offering than reducing your price. This can be hard in the beginning if you are not making many or any sales, but generally lack of sales could be due to many things, including:

> *You don't have enough traffic or the right people seeing your offer.* The more traffic you have, the more people will see your offers and potentially buy. Unfortunately this is something that grows over time, which means that when you are starting out you may not know if a lack of sales is a result of low traffic or something else. Either way, focusing on increasing the number of visitors and subscribers to your website is always beneficial to your business.

> *Your sales information or presentation is not compelling enough.* This can be a clincher! We have taken a product that was generating no sales, rewritten the copy and had sales within minutes of putting it up. Sales copy is an art form, and the better you become at it the more money you will make. This is an area where it is worth investing in courses and books to improve your skills, or in hiring a professional sales copywriter to produce your sales pages for you. Take an active interest in every piece of sales copy that finds its way to you; analyse what it is that makes it compelling (or not), analyse their calls to action and what language and images they use to create credibility.

> *Your sales information does not reflect a valuable offer for the price.* Your sales information needs to show the immense value that people will get from your product if they buy it. If you can break this down to time and money then do

that; quantify how much time, money or pain your product could save someone if they had this knowledge or training. Add bonuses that will be really useful to the customer, things that they can't get elsewhere. Make it a hugely valuable offer—an offer they can't refuse!

➼ *Your sales process is too complicated.* In the area of subscriptions and sales, less is more when it comes to number of processes. This is relatively easy to diagnose. Ask a few people to go to your website, make a purchase and then give you feedback on the process and suggest improvements you might make.

➼ *Your payment gateway or offer does not give confidence to buyers.* If people are even the slightest bit unsure about your payment application or your product, they won't buy. Again, to resolve this, ask people in your target market to go through your sales process and make suggestions about how you can improve it. For product-related concerns, consider adding a money-back guarantee to your sales information so that people can see that there is really no risk in buying your product.

There is no right answer when choosing a price; different people have different strategies. Generally, people new to selling tend to underprice themselves or heavily discount because of a lack of confidence or knowledge of the market. It is all part of the learning curve. If you are making sales, you know you are on the right track and you can always tweak your offers as you grow. The right price is the price that you can confidently sell at, and it really depends on your frame of mind. What really does help is getting testimonials and feedback from people who use your product. The more great feedback you get, the more confident you will feel about the value of your product, so if you need to spend a bit of time having people review your products then do that first. If you feel that your sale price should be higher than the amount you are comfortable with right now, create a time-limited discount so that people can see your actual price and have an incentive to buy at the discounted rate. This will give you a chance to test your prices and move up over time.

Marketing

When launching a new product, aim to have as many people as possible involved. The more people you can get promoting it, talking about it and having used it, the better. Asking other people or companies to help you promote your digital product and having a database of familiar people who would benefit from it provides you with the opportunity to launch your products with a flow of revenue from the beginning.

As you grow and network in your industry, you will open doors for partnerships and cross-promotion that will help you increase the visibility of your products as they launch. Get into the habit of thinking about who and what you can leverage when you are launching a new product. My clients are often surprised at the number of people they know or have access to who are keen to get involved.

Consider the different resources you currently have access to, or could potentially have access to if you were willing to make a few calls. Take out your notebook and write a list of people or companies you can approach from the following sources:

➪ your existing database and fans

➪ existing partnerships, sister websites and other bloggers you have developed relationships with

➪ social networks such as Twitter, Facebook and LinkedIn, and also other people who have large social networks who would be willing to post on your behalf. If you have 300 friends on Facebook and each of your friends has another 300 friends, overnight you have a potential 90 000 people who may see your post or click on your link

➪ owners of businesses with complementary services

➥ other business owners in the industry who would have a relevant database

➥ people who would really benefit from becoming an affiliate

➥ your family, friends, neighbours and colleagues (if you are still working!)

➥ forums that you frequent.

Once you are clear about what resources you have access to, create a plan for each one that will be attractive to those involved. People are often happy to help, and if they can't help in the way that you suggest, be bold and ask if they can think of other ways in which they can help you with your launch. The following table will help to give you some ideas.

People who may help with marketing	Opportunities for promotion
Friends	Promote through Facebook and Twitter, email their friends, etc.
1	
2	
etc.	
Business network	Review in their newsletter, link to/from their website, blog about, etc.
1	
2	
etc.	
Industry contacts	Co-brand product, offer a percentage of sales for promotion, etc.
1	
2	
etc.	
Other opportunities	Radio interview, press release, etc.
1	
2	
etc.	

Consider the potential reach of each possible resource; if they have a huge relevant database and you think they may be inundated with similar requests, think about what you can offer to make it attractive for them to get involved. Be different, and consider how you can use your launch to help them achieve their goals for their business.

Make the most of what you've got

Here are some suggestions for how you can be attractive to those who may promote you. This is not an exhaustive list but it gives you some initial ideas to start the creative juices flowing, so that you can make the most of what you have. There will be different opportunities for everyone depending on the topic, the type of product you are selling, who you already know and who you are bold enough to contact.

- Offer one main organisation an exclusive pre-release for their database with an increase in referral commission for a defined launch period.

- Invite everyone interested to register as an affiliate so that they get rewarded for any sales they refer to you.

- Offer free copies of your product to people you think may want to review it for their blog or website.

- If you have the opportunity to work with a large organisation with a big marketing engine, offer to co-brand the product and share in the profits.

- Offer a percentage of sales to a charity, school or not-for-profit in exchange for their help with promotion to their database.

- Give copies to other bloggers and companies that they can use as prizes.

- Contact local radio stations to see if they want to interview you and give away copies on the show.

✎ Offer a licence opportunity or exclusive member discount for the members of organisations that you work with.

In your notebook, make a list of anyone and everyone you can think of who you can contact, and then in a separate column write a list of everything you could do to get your product out there, using the list above as a guide.

Prior to the launch, ask everyone who has agreed to help promote you to market you and your site at least twice a week in the two weeks before the launch. Also remind them to continue to promote you for a week or two afterwards. Make it easy for them by providing emails, Tweets and Facebook text and links that they can cut and paste when they need them. Remind them each week on the days you want them to promote you. Keep people updated on the progress, and make sure you thank them profusely for being involved!

Automated payments and distribution

With payments and distribution the key is for your set up to be easy, cheap and reliable. For free products, MailChimp is great for distribution of digital products that come in document form. For paid products, PayPal will look after payments and E-Junkie will look after reporting, affiliates and distribution. This set up will give you buttons or shopping facilities on your website. When people click to purchase from your website, the E-Junkie button will take them to PayPal to manage the payment. In the background E-Junkie will note any affiliate connection to the sale and then provide thank you pages with links for distributing your products. You can customise each part of the sales process, even down to managing the number of times people can download using the link.

Once set up, you will have an automated system that will email you once new sales are completed. This automated set up is the key to smooth, low-maintenance internet sales, and leaves you to spend your time discovering the art of effectively marketing your website and products.

Case study: Grassroots Internet Strategy

Our first paid product was an eCourse: *Step-by-Step Website Planning for Start-Ups*. The reason we started with this product was because it was where we could potentially help people the most. The idea came from the sheer number of business owners who came to us with website problems because they didn't know what they needed to plan for before they started.

Because we worked in the industry and had worked one on one with people we had an idea about what problems we could solve, and so we were clear that this would be a useful product. We couldn't see any similar products in the market, or if they were there we couldn't find them in the search engines.

Although we planned for several products to be in the series, this one felt like the natural first choice, something that would give our customers a head start.

We had several people go through our products, at different times and for different reasons—some to proofread for flow, spelling and grammar, some in the industry to confirm the content and a few people who were our target customers. We also wanted to know how useful they found the product. At each stage we got feedback on how we could improve the course, and we were very happy with the result.

We were unsure of a price to start with and so we offered a discounted rate for the first three months while we worked on our traffic numbers and trialled different sales copy. Once we were happy that we could show the value we removed the discount.

Although our first sale was really exciting, sales were slow at first, which was disheartening until we realised that we just had to keep working on our database and traffic. Because we were a brand-new website, not many people were getting a chance to see our product offering. As our database and number of visitors grew so did our sales.

We found that our customers were very vocal about the product and were happy to let us use their photos for our testimonials, which added credibility to our sales pages. We also added a great guarantee, which not only gave them their money back if they were not satisfied but we would give them a free personal session as well.

Our sales copy is a work in progress; we still change things and test new things from time to time.

The wrap-up

🖎 Creating your own products will help establish your expertise as well as help towards achieving subscription goals or revenue goals.

🖎 Define the purpose of your product before you begin production.

🖎 Think about how you will capture the style and personality of your existing website and communications.

🖎 Be ruthless with editing, and also use the process to collect testimonials and reviews.

🖎 When choosing a price, consider the value of the information to the customer. If you are uncertain, try to increase the value of the offer over time rather than decreasing the price.

🖎 Make marketing a community effort and give people great reasons to get involved with your launch.

🖎 An automatic payment and distribution system must be low cost and reliable. You only want to be notified once the sale is complete.

Chapter 8

What's next?

So this is it. You have read the book, thought about your dream lifestyle, identified what lights your fire and how you can create an income on the internet. Now it's up to you! Now you get to put it all into practice. This is where the rubber hits the road, where you start creating value from the skills, knowledge and experiences you have had, the things that you are most passionate about. I have found the process to be exciting and humbling.

If you have gotten this far, you probably have a genuine interest in the idea that you can create a low-maintenance income based on something that you are passionate about — great! So what's next?

Get out there ... now! Yes ... *now!*

It's time to take action!

The next step is for you to step out and get started. If you are someone who needs to do a lot of research, get researching;

if you are someone who finds it hard to make decisions, get deciding; if you are someone who needs discipline, find some people to keep you on the straight and narrow. Whatever it's going to take to get you out of your comfort zone and catapulted into a new way of thinking, acting and working, do it *now* so you can reap the rewards of a lifestyle that lights your fire.

The only way to get good at something is to gain experience and put yourself out there. Along with commitment and determination, the success of your internet business will depend on your willingness to learn more and more about how to make your business successful (in creating value as well as marketing). You need to test what works and what doesn't work for the community you want to attract. If you have not done this before, there is only one way to find out—get started.

Clarify in your mind the goals you have for your lifestyle and look at what it would take for you to get there. If you are stuck on which internet topic to start with, go back over the exercises in the book and go with your gut instinct about what is right for you. Developing any skill, including how to create income on the internet, takes time and perseverance. If you are keen to start other blogs or websites or focus on other topics later then you will have the opportunity, so don't worry about getting *the one* first up. If you decide to explore more topics down the track they will build on what you learned from previous experiences. As we discussed, your passions and what you are interested in may change, but every day that you spend discovering how to build a successful business online will contribute to your overall effectiveness in generating low-maintenance income.

Remember to keep a level head when making decisions. If someone offers you an amazing opportunity to get hundreds of thousands of extra visitors, or earn thousands of dollars a day, be warned—there are many sharks out there! If it sounds too good to be true, it probably is.

The key to success for your business is to expand your community of like-minded people, work with an intention to create revenue and deliver consistently high quality content.

Your content will improve a lot as you learn and develop in your chosen industry, which is another good reason to start now.

Once you start to become familiar with the process and the tools that you use, you will naturally look to improve your systems, processes, presentation and delivery, so it is okay not to know what you are doing at first! The more willing you are to be patient and learn, the more you will achieve.

Although I have given you plenty to think about, this is just the beginning. Your path, what you learn and the opportunities that open up to you as a result will be uniquely yours.

You will never know how well you can do unless you are in the market, testing your theories and ideas. You will never know what you don't know until you hit up against it. Some of my biggest failures actually ended up shaping the path to my low-maintenance income, so I have nothing but appreciation for every part of the journey, especially for the really bumpy bits that helped me learn the most. It's not rocket science but it does take some work to get it right.

The benefit of an internet business is that your cost of start-up can be really low if you want it to be. The majority of the cost will be your time, and if you consider it training—training yourself in the art of creating a lifestyle-based income—you can have a lot of fun along the way.

There will be plenty of things that you may never figure out (or even want to), but that is not a reason not to start! Internet marketing is a huge beast and no individual can know everything. The internet, technology and new applications are so expansive and move on so quickly that it makes sense to get in as cheaply as possible and as soon as possible, and then upgrade as you learn and grow.

It is also important for this reason not to let your business stagnate. Even when you get it to a point where there is very little maintenance needed, keep abreast of internet technology, keep looking for opportunities to expand or improve, leverage what you have created and be nimble in your approach. Get involved in other website start-ups that interest you and be a generous member of the internet community. Once you have spent your time developing resources and a community, help others do the same. Always look for mutually beneficial partnerships and keep your offering fresh and innovative.

Because things can change so quickly on the internet, you need to keep your eye on the ball. Things will change rapidly around you, and depending on your industry this may mean your products need updating or replacing from time to time. When Twitter launched its new version, for example, we had to change all of the images in our eBook to reflect this. Things like this can happen with very little notice, so keep up! If you are relying on your business to maintain your lifestyle for a long time (say, from 20 to 70 years), keeping abreast of technology and industry changes becomes very important.

Are your goals big enough?

It can feel very uncomfortable to have a big goal with no idea how to achieve it, but it's okay to feel like this. In fact, I think this is a prerequisite for being an entrepreneur. The level to which you are willing to be uncomfortable will determine the size of the goals you dare to chase. This is the feeling that accompanies any major challenge and adventure, and it is what puts off many people from declaring and pursuing what they really want from life. Although I tend to focus on the positive aspects of everything, with each of my adventures I still sometimes experience a rollercoaster of feelings from adrenalin and excitement to fear and uncertainty.

Things worth having in life can be a challenge to achieve. Notice the thoughts in your head when it is time to take action; are you excited, scared, motivated or sceptical? Are these the same feelings you bring to other new challenges and opportunities? Are the positive thoughts enough to get you going? And keep you going? Are the negative ones powerful enough to stop you?

Don't let your emotions get in the way of taking the necessary actions to achieve your dream lifestyle. I used to be terrified of public speaking. The fear stopped me from ever putting my hand up in group situations. I let the fear be so overwhelming that I would miss out on opportunities and kick myself afterwards. I wanted to speak but I felt I just couldn't. Then I was offered the opportunity to host a radio show and I was aching to do it, but I let fear stop me for over a year. One day I realised it was crazy not to try, so I took a deep breath and set it up with the station manager. I was still scared, but I did it anyway. I would love to say that my fear dissipated immediately, but it didn't. I would shake every time I spoke for nearly six months! Two years later, I have a show that is one of the highlights of my week. It has opened up many doors for me and I now feel much more confident expressing myself.

Am I still scared of public speaking? Yes! Although I feel quite comfortable on the radio, I still shake, break out in a cold sweat and can't breathe when speaking in front of a group or a video camera. But, I take every opportunity I can to practise.

In the last few years I have taken on challenges that make me very uncomfortable, and as a result I have grown, learnt and achieved far more than any other time in my life. After I take on these challenges, I often feel revitalised, energised and silly, like a young kid again! What makes me do this is my hunger to learn and absorb everything I possibly can so I can get the most out of life.

Creating a fulfilling life

My intention with this retirement challenge was to retire from my need to be working five days a week to create income. It was not to retire from doing anything ever again. There is nothing wrong with wanting to have the freedom to spend each day on the beach or watch daytime TV … but, after a while the novelty wears off and we crave fulfilment in other ways.

What we each consider to be fulfilling is different, and it may change from month to month or year to year. Whether you are fulfilled by striving to be better at something, making a difference to people, bringing up children, being creative, inventing things, being an explorer or standing up as a public figure, everything requires some effort; an investment of your time and energy.

Our need for fulfilment is ongoing. You don't find hugely successful people sitting around satisfied that they are done. More often than not they are out there looking for the next challenge, the next journey or the next adventure. As long as there is life in your bones, you will yearn to do things that fulfil you.

Having the freedom to explore this gives me a whole new set of motivators. But, instead of being motivated by money, I am now motivated by creativity, curiosity and a want to use my skills to help people less fortunate than myself.

The biggest shifts for me have been internal. Being removed from the stress of commuting, traffic, early morning wake ups, being target driven, boring meetings and suits, I have found that life has become very simple, and as a result I am content and happy. I am much more aware of and focused on my health. I have time to cook healthy and tasty food a few times a day and exercise when the mood takes me. I only work with people if I think they are amazing, and often go to the beach for a few hours each day, mid-week when it is deliciously empty.

Life's lessons

Every challenge you face along the way presents opportunities to learn more about yourself and the world around you. Here are a few of the lessons I have learned on my journey.

The more I have to do, the more I'm able to achieve

I have always been a busy person, but year after year I take on more and more and achieve more and more. If I wrote a weekly to-do list now and gave it to myself five years ago, I would have deemed it impossible (or at least crazy). Working smarter and not harder is definitely a requirement of success.

It is okay to be fallible

We live in a world of keeping up appearances and looking good. For a perfectionist like me, it is still very scary to present myself warts'n'all to the general public. What I have found, however, is that my most honest and vulnerable blogs are the ones that seem to be the most popular. People don't want you to be perfect, they want you to be human, and humans (however much we would like to be) are not perfect.

Take responsibility for what you are creating

Whether you like it or not, you attract the results, relationships and situations that you find yourself in. You really are that powerful. Even if you hate a situation, the familiarity of that situation will have you seek it out over and over again. So, take a look at those recurring arguments you have with your partner, the annoying problems you have with your kids, family, boss, bank, utilities company, bus driver, pets, neighbours … whatever. Look at the things that really bite that seem to happen over and over and see if you can spot how you are causing them to happen. Consider what it is about you that attracts those familiar situations and challenge yourself to get a different result.

The happier you are the less you care about *stuff*

The life flashing before you as you take your last breath will no doubt consist of both warm and regretful memories of love, relationships and adventures had or not had—and that's it. I doubt very much that you will be mourning your expensive shoes the dog ate, or that time you missed out on getting a new version of the iPhone on launch day. I still like to dress to kill from time to time and make the most of technological advances, but the quantity of these so-called needs has diminished significantly as my feeling of fulfilment grows; there is no comparison to getting genuine pleasure from your achievements in life.

Be creative in having what you want

I believe that if you get a no when you ask for something, you haven't asked in the right way, you haven't asked enough times or you haven't asked the right person. If you take on this attitude you will find that your luck will improve!

If something is worth having or is essential to the success of your project, business or goal, then you need to treat the process with respect, creativity and confidence. It helps also if you are open to the suggestion that anything is possible! When asking for something you want, make sure you ask with the level of enthusiasm you had when you first conceived of the project. Bring this energy to every conversation and the people you're asking will salivate at the thought of helping you achieve your goal.

The destination is only a place to get to; it is the journey that counts

This makes sense to me every time I realise that I have forgotten it! Sometimes I spend so much time worrying about the goal, the result and the success that I can lose sight of the fact that every moment is the bit that actually matters.

If you don't spend some time each day appreciating what you have, it may be time to shift your focus. Because all you have is what you have right now ... and now ... and now ...

Over to you!

There you have it. You now understand how you can create an alternative source of income that you could—if you are moti-vated—set up in 12 months.

I hope I have planted some seeds. At the back of the book you'll find a list of the websites of the people and companies that I have mentioned, as well as a list of additional resources for really making the most of this opportunity. The rest is up to you.

So...

You want to create an alternative source of low-maintenance income...

You want to spend your time working on the things that you are most passionate about...

You want to create financial, time and geographical freedom with your work...

Here is the big question...

What's next?

Thanks for reading, good luck, have fun and enjoy the ride.

Glossary

Affiliate marketing   An arrangement to promote someone else's product or service on your website or to your database. When people click through from your website or email and purchase a product you are paid a commission on that sale.

CMS   Content management system—software that manages the administration of the content on your website, such as the text and images on each page.

Copyright   Exclusive rights granted to the author or creator of an original work, including the right to sell, copy, distribute and adapt the work. Copyright can be transferred to another person or entity.

CPA	Cost per action—the website owner is paid when someone clicks on an advert they have placed on the website and takes the required action, such as purchasing or subscribing.
CPC	Cost per click—you make a certain amount of money when someone clicks on an advert on your site.
Email marketing	The act of sending an email to a list of recipients for marketing purposes, such as promoting an offer, newsletter, blog, event or new article.
ISP	Internet service provider—a company that offers its clients access to the internet through a variety of means, including dial-up, cable and wireless.
Open source	The practice of collaborative production and development of software, giving the public free access to the product and materials.
PDF	Portable document format—the best format for distributing documents that are designed to be read only.
Plugins	Software components that you 'plug in' to your website, adding all manner of features and customisation options.
Podcast	Audio or video files that are downloaded through applications such as iTunes; usually released in episodes.
PR	Public relations—the management of communication between you and the public. The goal of PR is to increase the

amount of communication delivered, so that you get as much exposure as possible.

SEM   Search engine marketing—you pay to advertise your website on a search engine results page. In Google, this means appearing in what is called the Ads section.

SEO   Search engine optimisation—the art of optimising your website for search engines to help it appear higher in search engine results. Well-executed SEO will make your website visible to more people who search for related products, services and information.

SMM   Social media marketing—the use of social networks, including Facebook, Twitter and LinkedIn, for marketing, sales, public relations and customer service.

Spam   The outlawed practice of using electronic messaging systems such as email to send unsolicited marketing messages.

Tags   Keywords or terms assigned to a piece of information (like an internet bookmark, image or file). Tags help describe an item and allow it to be found again when browsing or searching. Tags are generally chosen informally and personally by the item's creator.

URL   Uniform resource locator—an identifier that specifies where a specific resource is available on the internet as well as the mechanism for retrieving it. The most common usage of URLs is for the addresses of web pages.

Web hosts

Companies that provide space on a server (computer, or series of computers) that allows website owners to make their website available via the internet.

Webinar

A live seminar that is held on the internet, generally consisting of audio and either video or screen share. Participants may or may not be able to converse with the presenter.

Web traffic

The measure of the number of visitors to a website and the number of pages they visit.

Useful resources

CallBurner Application you can download to record calls you make using Skype. <www.callburner.com>

ClickBank The internet's leading retailer of digital products, whether you're looking to sell, promote or shop for digital goods. <www.clickbank.com>

cPanel A website management application that gives end users server administration access. <www.cpanel.net>

E-Junkie A service that provides shopping cart and buy now buttons, in-house affiliate programs, automated download delivery and more for selling digital or tangible goods on your website. <www.e-junkie.com>

Flowplayer	Flash-based application that allows you to stream video from your website. <www.flowplayer.org>
Google Ads	Helps connect you with potential customers by placing relevant ads on the right-hand side of search results pages. <www.adwords.google.com>
Google Analytics	A free web application that allows you to monitor the behaviour of visitors on your website. <www.google.com/analytics>
HostGator	The best value web hosting for bloggers, including WordPress auto-installer 'QuickInstall'. <www.hostgator.com>
How to retire in 12 months	My blog, packed with heaps of valuable information and resources, along with regular updates on what I'm up to. <www.retireyoung.com.au>
MailChimp	An easy-to-use email marketing service that is free if you have fewer than 2000 subscribers. <www.mailchimp.com>
PayPal	An e-commerce business facility that allows users to make payments and transfer money via the internet. <www.paypal.com>
Skype	An application that allows users to make voice calls over the internet as well as instant messaging, file transfer and video conferencing. <www.skype.com>
SourceBottle	A free online service that connects journalists with sources. <www.sourcebottle.com.au>

VodBurner   An application that will let you record and edit Skype video chats and conferences and post them straight to YouTube. <www.vodburner.com>

WordPress   An open source content management system (CMS), often used as a blog publishing application. WordPress is the most popular CMS in use today. <www.wordpress.org>

WordPress Plugins   Small applications developed by external developers specifically to extend the functionality of WordPress. You will find the menu of available plugins in the plugins menu in the WordPress dashboard.

Website examples

~~~~~~~~~~~~~~~~~~~~~~~~~~~~~~~~~~~~~~~

Here is a list of the website examples mentioned throughout the book, some large, some small. Visit them to see the techniques they use for their passion-based businesses. Don't be afraid to note what you don't like and copy what you do like from each website. Subscribe to their blogs or newsletters and analyse what they send you.

☞ Divine Write <www.divinewrite.com>

☞ The Essence of Breastfeeding <www.the-essence-of-breastfeeding.com>

☞ Flying Solo <www.flyingsolo.com.au>

☞ Grassroots Internet Strategy <www.grassrootsinternetstrategy.com.au>

☞ Happyzine <www.happyzine.co.nz>

☞ How to retire in 12 months—resources <www.retireyoung.com.au> (password for book resources: passion99)

➪ Innovative Passive Income <www.innovativepassiveincome.com>

➪ Jessica Van Den <www.jessicavanden.com>

➪ Joy of Quotes <www.joyofquotes.com>

➪ Kty West Pet Portraits <www.ktywest.co.uk>

➪ Laura Kate Australia <www.laurakateaustralia.com>

➪ Logan Dance Sydney <www.logandancesydney.com.au>

➪ Man vs Debt <www.manvsdebt.com>

➪ Market Angel <www.marketangel.com.au>

➪ Moving 2 London <www.moving2london.com>

➪ Moving 2 Sydney <www.moving2sydney.com>

➪ Oh My Giddy Aunt <www.ohmygiddyaunt.com.au>

➪ ProBlogger <www.problogger.net>

➪ Publicity Express <www.publicityexpress.com.au>

➪ The Smart Passive Income Blog <www.smartpassiveincome.com>

➪ Sober Paddy <www.soberpaddy.com>

Index

12 months 69
— reason for 4–5

advertising space 80–81
affiliate marketing 83–86, 90–91,
  110–111, 113, 123, 127, 147
— commissions and 84
— laws relating to 114
— selecting products for 85–86
analysis paralysis 43–45
annual leave 14
anti-spam laws 109
anything is possible 48–51
audio products 139–140
automated payments and
  distribution 147
Avaaz 86

blogs 1, 35, 70–76, 79, 96,
  106–111, 113–114, 130
— creating personality for
  103–106
— ideas for 71–76
— naming 104–105
— online relationships and 71
— reasons for creating 70–71
— updating regularly 71,
  99–100
— websites for 106–107

CallBurner 139–140
call to action 89, 98
case studies 114–115
challenging yourself 60–61
charities 120

Cheap Australian Domains 105
ClickBank 85, 110
co-authoring 132
commissions 83–85, 119
communication 59–60
competition 94–96
competitions 82, 99
content management system
    (CMS) 106–107
content marketing 112–115
cost per action (CPA) 83
cost per click (CPC) 83

database *see* subscriber database
dating websites 87
discipline 10, 20
Divine Write 130
domain names 105–106
donations 86–87
dream lifestyle 5, 19, 23, 25–26,
    30, 48, 61, 64, 151

eBooks 38, 82, 137, 138
    —providing free 100
    —writing 130–133
eCourses 131, 139
E-Junkie 88, 110, 138, 147
Elance 132
email marketing 98, 115–116
    —automating 109
Essence of Breastfeeding 134
expert panel formula 134–135

Facebook 101, 111–112, 122,
    132, 144
failure 32, 35, 52, 55–57, 65
    —learning from 56–57
fear 155
    —chemical trickery and 45–47
    —putting in perspective 47–48

Flowplayer 140
Flying Solo 81, 87–88
forums 122, 123
Freelance Switch 132

General Masses 65–66
generating sales leads 89–90, 118
generosity 57–58
get-rich-quick schemes 9–10, 64
ghost writing 132
global financial crisis 8
goals 9, 23–26, 48–49, 152,
    154–155
    —deadlines and 68–70
    —money and 23–25
    —passions and 67–70
    —retirement and 14
good life crisis 26–28, 65
Google 107, 113, 116, 117–118
    —AdSense 83–84
    —AdWords 123
    —Analytics 96–97, 123
government 8
Grassroots Internet Strategy
    15–16, 75
    —anything is possible 49–50
    —creation of 1–2
    —marketing and 122–124
    —product creation and 137,
        148–149
    —providing value and 97
    —revenue generation and
        90–91
    —value creation and 34–35,
        40–41
guest blogging 113, 119–120, 123
gut feeling *see* intuition

Happyzine 38, 82, 140
hoplinks 85

income
—increases in 24–25
—supplementing 14–15
Innovative Passive Income 96
intentions, declaring publicly 10
internet
—communities 33, 35, 36, 79,
111, 129, 152, 154
—number of users 8, 13, 73, 80
—searches on 73
internet-based business
—expertise and 19, 35–40
—getting started 12–14,
26–29, 151–154
—honesty and 37
—ideas for 71–76
—naming 104–105
—passions and 70–71
—requirements for 13
—start-up costs of 12–14, 153
—trial and error 91
—upgrading over time 13,
106, 111
intuition 58–61

jargon 133
Joy of Quotes 73

keywords 96, 108, 113, 116–118

Laura Kate Australia 140
life's lessons 156–158
LinkedIn 101, 111–112, 122,
132
listening skills 59–60
low-maintenance income
2, 9–10, 79–102, 153
—getting started 12–14
—versus passive income 11–12
luck 53

MailChimp 109, 116, 147
Man vs Debt 104
Market Angel 38
marketing 81, 144–147
—resources for 146
membership programs 85
money
—effect on people 3, 23–25
—freedom and 24–25, 29
—goals and 23–25, 29–31
—lifestyle and 19–42
motivation 10–11, 27
—deadlines and 10–11, 68–70
—money and 29–31
Moving 2 London 37, 82
multi-level marketing 30

networking 121–122
newsletters 99, 121
—automating 109

oDesk 132
Oh My Giddy Aunt 72
online relationships 71

paid add-value services 87–88
paid employment
—leaving 15
—personal value and 31–32
—promotions and 24–25
paid membership 87–88
parents 15, 36
partnerships 118–120, 130
passion personality 64–67
passions 12, 14, 25
—creating a business from
9, 19
—finding 63–78
—importance of 30, 63–64
Passion Seekers 64–65

passive income versus low-
maintenance income 11–12
payment applications 109–110
PayPal 86, 88, 109–110, 147
peers, opinions of 36
persistence 51–53, 152
personal fulfilment 12, 14–15,
19–42, 155–156
press releases 120, 123
ProBlogger 130
procrastination 44
product or service reviews
113–114
products 88–89
— accessibility of 133
— creating your own 127–149
— editing 141
— formulae for 133–136
— packaging 137–141
— pricing 142–144
— purpose of 128–130
— style of 131
— writing 130–133
product/service bundles 119
product/service samples 99
Publicity Express 100
public relations (PR) 118,
120–121, 123

referrals 118–120
retirement 7–17
— goals for 14
— new approach to 8–9
— saving and 8
— traditional view of 7–8

Safe Operators 65–66
sales, lack of 142–143
search engine marketing (SEM)
117–118

search engine optimisation (SEO)
116–117
search engines, organic listings in
113–114
selective hearing 53–55
selling yourself 103–125
Smart Passive Income Blog, The
38
Sober Paddy 104
social media marketing 111–112
social media networks 101
spam 109
sponsorship 81–82
stand-down periods 85
step-by-step guides 136
students 15
subscriber database 80, 84
— building 97–101, 128
— communicating with 86, 121
— importance of 71, 97–98
— incentives for 82, 93,
108–109
success mindset 43–62
superannuation 7
— global financial crisis and 8

taking action 50–51
testimonials 114–115, 141
time motivators 10–11
title tag 117
top tips formula 135–136
Twitter 101, 111–112, 132, 144

value 31–41, 92–94
— creating 19, 33–41, 71–76
— judging 92–93
— methods of providing 93–94
— perceptions of 31–33
— personal experiences and
36–41

video blogs 114
video products 140–141

web seminars 100–101
websites
—age of 117
—analysing 92–93
—analysing visitor behaviour
96–97
—competitors 34
—copy for 89, 107–108,
142–143
—creating personality for
103–106
—design of 107
—essentials for 106–110
—hosting for 108
—marketing 111–122
—naming 104–105
—number of links 117
—number of subscribers 91
—number of visitors 80, 84,
91, 98, 142
—optimising 116–117
—page titles 117
—payment process 143
—sales process 143
—size of 117
—upgrading over time 13,
106, 111
what's next? 52, 151–159
WordPress 107, 108
—plugins for 109, 116, 123
worksheets 5